재미교포 **장재옥** 여사의 30년 요리연구 !

A thirty-year study by Korean-American immigrant,
Ms.Jae-ok Chang

우리요리 이야기
Vignette of Korean Cooking

Cooking....

의 사인 남편을 따라 American Dream을 가지고 이 낯선 땅에 이민온 지 30여년이 되었습니다. 이민 초기에는 외로움으로 고국을 그리워했고 그 후에도 튼튼한 뿌리를 이 미국땅에 내리기 위한 바쁜 생활 가운데 틈틈이 고국을 그리워 했으며 근래에도 안정된 생활속에서 지난 날을 돌아보며 고국을 그리워합니다.

그러나 한편으론 우리 자녀들로 하여금 Korean-American의 특수한 입장을 깊이 깨닫게 하고 뿌리를 찾아서 이해하고 그것을 잘 보존하며 지켜나가도록 도움을 주는 부모가 되기를 기도합니다.

그러기 위해서는 한국말을 가르쳐 한국의 문화를 이해하도록 하고 또 한국음식에 익숙하게 함으로써 한국의 전통을 이해할 수 있도록 도와주기를 원합니다.

저는 평범한 주부로서 요리를 전공한 적은 없습니다만, 내 사랑하는 딸 Barbara(바바라)에게 한국의 전통을 물려주기 위해서 이 책을 씁니다.

저는 아주 어릴 적부터 음식에 굉장히 관심이 있었고, 취미가 있었습니다. 한 가지 음식을 보면 열 가지 이상의 아이디어가 생겼습니다. 어떤 음식이든 예사로 보지 않았고 반드시 해 보는 열성이 있었습니다. 이곳에서 취미로 해 본 요리들을 가지고 이 곳 주위에 있는 여러 한인 사회단체들의 요청에 따라 20년 이상 요리 강습회 강사로 강의한 자료들을 모아서 부족하지만 이렇게 책으로 엮어서 딸 Barbara에게 주기로 작정했습니다.

그래서 이 책에는 아주 기초적인 음식의 요리법도 포함시켰고 또한 이 곳 동양 식품점이나 서양식품점에서 구할 수 있는 재료들을 써서 요리할 수 있도록 이 책을 기록했으며 화학조미료를 쓰지 않았으며 가능하면 지방질이 적게 들어가도록 노력했습니다. 우리 자녀 2세들과 미국 사람들로 쉽게 우리 음식을 즐길 수 있도록 요리과정을 상세하게 한국말과 영어로 기록했습니다.

이 책이 발간되기까지 많은 분들이 수고하시고 도와 주셨습니다. 특히 말없이 걱정하며 협조하고 조언을 해 주신 남편께 감사드리며 영어번역을 위해 수고해 주신 Mrs. Young Vipond 그리고 자료를 교정해 주시고 타이프를 맡아주신 Mrs. 김무환씨에게 정말 감사드립니다.

또한 한국의 출판사 관계의 일과 그외 여러가지 일로 수고해 주신 남편 친구되시는 한국에 계신 편영식 박사님 부부, 이 책을 낼 때까지 용기와 격려를 주신 김영환 박사님 부부, 조남제 박사님 부부와 구본철 박사님 부부께 진심으로 감사드립니다. 사실 이 책은 저의 평범한 지혜로 썼으며 정말 사랑하는 후세의 장래 식생활이나 또한 한국의 전통을 이해하는데 조금이라도 도움이 되고 한국음식에 관심있는 미국 주부들에게 도움이 된다면 더없는 기쁨이 되겠습니다. 부족한 저에게 요리책을 쓸 수 있도록 능력과 지혜를 주신 하나님께 감사 드립니다.

It has been almost thirty years since my physician husband and I moved to this unfamiliar land from Korea, immigrating with the American Dream. At first, I was lonely and longed for my homeland all the time. However, as we settled and busily established ourselves in America, I began to think of Korea from time to time. Nowadays, I cherish the past and think fondly of my homeland.

I pray that I can be a helpful parent who can teach our children how unique they are as Korean-Americans and how to preserve their heritage. I think it is necessary to teach them the Korean language and familiarize them with traditional Korean cuisine in order to create an understanding of the Korean culture and its customs.

Although I am simply a housewife and mother who has not received formal training in cooking, I have written this cookbook for my lovely daughter, Barbara, to pass on the Korean tradition. Ever since I was a young girl, I have been interested in food and have enjoyed cooking. When I thought of one dish, I would think of more than ten different ways to prepare it. I scrutinized every dish and always attempted to prepare everything I tasted.

For over twenty years, I have been giving cooking lessons and demonstrations upon the request of a number of Korean organizations in the greater Cleveland area. This cookbook is based on the research and recipes involved in the teaching process. As amateur and modest as it may be, I decided to create this book and dedicate it to my only daughter, Barbara. Throughout this book, I employ very rudimentary cooking methods and recipes that consist of ingredients that can easily be purchased at local oriental groceries and markets. I do not use any chemical food additives nor do I use any mono sodium glutamate in any of the recipes. I always use a minimal amount of fat when choosing the ingredients. I chose to write a bilingual cookbook for the sake of westerners who are interested in Korean cuisine and most importantly, for the generations to come of our children who may not read Korean.

This book could not have been published without the help of many people. First, I would like to thank my supportive husband who has always advised me and quietly supported me. I would also like to take this opportunity to thank the following individuals for making this cookbook possible: Mrs. Young Vipond for her translation and Mrs. Moo Hwan Kim for the typing and editing of the text. I would also like to show my sincere appreciation to our friends, Dr. and Mrs. Young Shik Pyun, for helping me with the publication and a variety of other important tasks in Korea. I will never forget the individuals who encouraged me and provided mental support throughout the whole process: Dr. and Mrs. Nam Je Cho, Dr. and Mrs. Bon Chul Koo, and Dr. and Mrs. Young Hwan Kim. I instinctively wrote this book in order to help our children prepare Korean food and understand our customs and traditions. It would also bring me great joy to know that this book can be of help to any American housewife who is interested in Korean cuisine. Finally, I would like to thank God for granting me the necessary wisdom and enabling me to write this cookbook.

Ms. Jae Ok Chang
Cleveland, Ohio

"보기에 아름답고 격조있는 요리"
"일상식탁에 오를 수 있는 요리"

그간 미국Ohio주의 Cleveland를 중심으로 여러지역의 한인회와 교회 등에서 요리강습을 주관하시던 장재옥 선생께서 요리에 대한 책을 출판하신데 대하여 진심으로 축하드립니다. 장선생의 요리솜씨는 이 지역에서는 이미 널리 알려져 있으며 요리강습때마다 여러 사람들의 감탄과 칭송을 받은지 오래입니다. 그의 음식은 "건강을 위한 요리", "맛있는 요리", "보기에 아름답고 격조있는 요리" 그리고 "일상식탁에 오를 수 있는 요리"여야 된다는 큰 과제를 가지고 연구되고 개발된 것들입니다. 특히 이번 책에는 영어와 한국어로 병기되게 함으로써 재미2세들에게 할머니와 어머니들의 손으로 만들어졌던 맛있고 멋있는 고국의 요리들을 배우고 만들수 있게 하며 고국의 맛을 이어받을 수 있는 큰 계기가 될 것을 확신하며 이 책을 모든 가정에 추천하는 바입니다. 그리고 이런 아름답고 유익한 책을 펴내신 장재옥 선생께 다시 한 번 감사드립니다.

미국 Ohio에서 Dong Sung Lee, M.D., ph.D.

First of all, I offer my genuine congratulation to Ms. Jae-ok Chang for publishing this cookbook after making her cooking lessons available to Korean communities and churches of the greater Cleveland area in Ohio. Around here it is a well-known fact that she is highly praised for her cooking talents and lessons. She has researched, created and developed her dishes with the following objectives over the years : "healthy and nutritional recipes", "delicious recipes", "esthetically pleasing recipes" and "everyday, easy-to-make recipes".
I highly recommend this bilingual cookbook especially for our second and future generations of Korean-Americans to learn and enjoy those dishes that were home-cooked by their mothers and grandmothers, and for giving our future generations an opportunity to inherit their motherland's unique cuisine and tastes. Again, I offer my sincere appreciation to Ms. Chang for writing this beautiful and helpful cookbook.

Dong Sung Lee, M.D., Ph.D.
Youngstown, Ohio

축 · 천 · 의 · 글

요리강습과 지면을 통하여 흔한 재료로 맛과 멋과
영양이 가득하고 다채 다향한 새로운 음식을 연구...

장재옥 여사는 20년이 넘도록 미국 오하이오주 클리블랜드 한인사회에 민족적 선각자로서 식생활 발전과 개선에 앞장섰다. 요리강습과 지면을 통하여 흔한 재료로 맛과 멋과 영양이 가득하고 다채다양한 새로운 음식을 연구, 교육, 보급하셨다.
클리블랜드 한인사회에 끼친 장재옥 여사의 봉사활동이 특출하기에 1999년도에는 한인회로부터 표창이 수여되었다. 장재옥 여사께서 금번 처음으로 한글과 영문으로 된 「우리요리 이야기」 이란 저서를 내는 것은 우리사회가 오랫동안 기다리고 바랬던 일이다. 장재옥 여사께 축하드리며 앞으로 이 책이 세계의 여성들과 가까워져서 쉽고 간단하게 짧은 시간을 들여 맛과 멋과 영양이 풍부한 요리로 건강한 가정, 건강한 사회를 만드는데 이바지하기를 바란다.

한인회장 오세근

For more than twenty years, Ms. Jae-ok Chang pioneered in improving and developing our cooking and eating habits in the Korean American community of the greater Cleveland, Ohio. With her cooking demonstrations and recipes, she educated and introduced to the community at large various dishes that are full of taste, beauty and nutritional value, and easy to make with commonly available ingredients.
The Korean American Association of the Greater Cleveland had recognized and honored Ms. Chang in 1999 for her outstanding contribution to Korean community. We have been waiting and hoping so long for her to publish a cookbook in both Korean and English.
I congratulate Ms. Chang, and hope that her book will available to people all over the world so that many more families can also enjoy simple and easy-to-make recipes for healthier families and communities in the near future.

Se Keun Oh, President
The Korean American Association of the greater Cleveland

한식의 전승과 계발에 노력하여 오신 장재옥 여사님 ...

장재옥 여사는 타고난 요리감각에 30여년간의 미주생활에서 몸소 체험한 경험을 접합시켜서 한식의 전승과 계발에 노력하여 오던 바 이번에 발간된 요리집은 이의 집성판이다. 이 책으로써 장여사는 1세들에게는 향수에 젖은 음식을, 2세들에게는 격조있는 한식요리법을, 그리고 외국인들에게는 새로운 식성을 찾아볼 수 있게 하였다.

이재원 클리블랜드 주립대 교수

Ms. Jae-ok Chang has combined her extraordinary cooking senses, thirty years of personal experimentation with food while living in the United States and development of more contemporary Korean recipes to make this cookbook a possibility. With this book she has provided a source for comfort food for the first generation immigrants, more authentic cooking methods for Korean food for the second generation and novel taste and cuisine for non-Korean readers.

Jae Won Lee, Professor
Cleveland State University, Cleveland, Ohio

추 · 천 · 의 · 글

아주 정교하고 예술적인 솜씨를 소유한 분이십니다

나의 마지막 20년간의 목회사역에 있어서, 장재옥 권사님을 동역자로 또는 협조자로, 같이 일하게 된 것을 하나님께 감사합니다. 장권사님은 천부(天賦)의 은사로서 아주 정교하고 예술적인 솜씨를 소유한 분이십니다. 요리하는 일, 꽃꽂이 하는 일, 그 외에도 집안장식을 하는 일에 있어서 탁월한 재능을 소유하셨고, 이 재능을 가지고 교회와 한인사회를 위하여 지대한 공헌을 해왔습니다.
이번에 그의 솜씨를 책에 담아서 귀한 요리책을 발간하게 된 것을 진심으로 축하합니다. 아무쪼록 이 책이 많은 가정주부들에게 큰 도움이 되며 더 나아가서 한국요리의 특이성을 국제사회에 널리 알리게 하는 뜻깊은 계기가 되기를 간절히 소원합니다.

한인 중앙장로교회 원로목사 구영환 Ph. D.

For the last twenty years of my service as a minister, I thank God for having Ms. Jae-ok Chang as my helper and co-worker. Our heavenly Father blessed her with artistic senses and talented hands. She possesses superb talents in cooking, flower arrangements, and interior design among many other things, and greatly served the church and Korean American community of the greater Cleveland with those special gifts. I sincerely congratulate her in publishing this cookbook. I wish and pray that this book will not only help many housewives, but also become a tool for showcasing unique Korean cuisine to international communities.

John Younghwan Koo, Ph.D., Pastor-Emeritus
The Korean Central Presbyterian Church of Cleveland

장재옥 여사님께서 만드는 맛있는 한국음식을
먹을수 있게 된것을 다행이라 생각합니다

제가 25년전 이 병원에서 일을 시작할 때 부터 Dr. Kwon과 Mrs. Kwon을 알게 되었습니다.
저희들의 직장에서는 맡은 일을 잘 수행하기 위하여 회식이 자주 있습니다.
그때마다 Mrs. Kwon께서는 정말 맛있는 순수한 한국음식을 대접해 줍니다. Mrs. Kwon께서는 정말 훌륭한 재능을 지니고 있는 분입니다. 지금도 우리과에 같이 일하는 모든 사람들이 Mrs. Kwon이 우리를 위해서 한국음식을 만들어 달라고 Dr. Kwon에게 간청합니다.
저희들은 Mrs. Kwon께서 만드는 맛있는 한국 음식을 먹을 수 있게 된것을 정말 다행이라고 생각합니다.

Maria Schmidt
Director, Medical Imaging

Working at Geauga Regional Hospital I became acquainted with Dr. Kwon and subsequently his wife 25 years ago. Our department has numerous parties as a team-building tool so to enhance this project Dr. Kwon volunteered his wife's authentic Korean cooking. What a gift to our staff!! I have never tasted better Korean food. Mrs. Kwon has an enviable talent.
Now whenever we get together, we all beg Dr. Kwon to have his wife make something for us.

Maria Schmidt
Director, Medical Imaging

추 • 천 • 의 • 글

어떤 화학 조미료도 쓰지않고
순수한 재료로 진미를 내는 요리 ...

2000년을 맞은 지금에 와서 관찰해 보면 인류가 드디어 영양식과 건강식에 관심을 가지고 어떻게 하면 건강하게 또 이상적인 체중을 유지할 수 있을까, 노력하며 또 그 목적달성을 위해서 달리는 그런 때가 바야흐로 온 것 같습니다.
이 책의 저자가 바로 그런 사람들 중에 대표적인 한사람으로 볼 수 있습니다.
저자는 자신의 체중과 건강을 식이요법과 규칙적인 에어로빅 운동으로 잘 조정하면서 하나님께서 주신 재능인 무궁무진한 요리솜씨로 늘 교회를 중심해서 또 사회봉사를 즐기는 분이며 이번에 특별히 수십, 수백가지의 요리를 연구 집필하는데 맛나니(MSG)나 그 이외의 어떤 화학 조미료도 전혀 쓰지 않고 순수한 재료로 진미를 내는 방법을 연구해서 쓴 점에 참 매력이 있다고 봅니다.
건강식과 영양식에 관심이 있는 현대인들은 한권쯤 가지고 실천에 옮겨 볼 만한 걸작품이 되리라고 믿습니다.

영양사 이정은

As we face the new millennium in the year 2000, the time has finally arrived for mankind to be concerned with nutritional and healthy eating habits as objectives, and to stay fit and maintain ideal weight. The author of this book, Ms. Jae-ok Chang, ideally represents this growing philosophy.
The author has not only maintained her ideal weight and good health by eating right and regularly engaging in aerobic exercise, but also used her tremendous cooking talents in serving the community mainly through her church.
This cookbook is especially attractive to me because none of the numerous recipes use any chemical food additives such as monosodium glutamate. I believe that this book will be a source for success to anyone who wants to switch to healthy and nutritional eating.

Jane Lee Han, RD, LD
Registered, Licensed and Consulting Dietitian.

목회 현장에서 만난 장재옥 권사님은
이웃에 유익을 주는 요리강사...

빠르게 변화하는 지구촌의 삶이 한결같이 인스턴트 식품을 선호하는 세상이 되었습니다. 허나 식탁에 오를 먹거리를 준비하는 주부의 정성어린 손놀림처럼 창조적이며 빛나는 손길이 있을까요? 세상이 온통 근본적인 변화에 당황해 한다고 한들 가족과 자신의 건강을 위해 맛나는 먹거리를 준비하는 주부들의 분주함은 예나 변함없이 위대한 것임이 틀림없습니다.

다양한 복합문화 환경에서 매주일마다 신령한 영(靈)의 음식을 준비해야 하는 이민 목사로서 영양가 좋고, 맛나는 식탁(設敎)을 생각하며 여러 자료들과 재료를 마련키 위해 東西古今의 요긴한 자료들을 참고하곤 합니다. 이때마다 가족의 건강과 행복을 염려하는 주부의 마음을 가까이 읽을 수 있었습니다.

목회 현장에서 만난 장재옥 권사님은 바로 이런 목회자의 심정을 가지시고 주부로 때로는 이웃에 유익을 주는 요리강사로 오랫동안 헌신하신 분이십니다. 금번에 장 권사님께서는 오랜 자신의 경험과 확신을 기반으로 미국에 사는 이민 1세만이 아니라 이민 2세들에게도 유익한, 고유의 전통어린, 품위 있고 실제로 영양가 있으며 맛나는 식탁준비의 자료와 조리법(Recipe)을 정리하시어 귀한 책자를 한영본으로 내놓으셨음을 기쁘게 생각합니다. 이 귀중한 결실이 1세들 뿐만 아니라 특별히 자라나는 이민 2세, 3세들에게 좋은 선물이 되기를 기대하면서 이 책을 즐거운 마음으로 추천하고자 합니다.

클리블랜드 중앙장로교회 담임목사 강기석

We are living in a fast-changing world that constantly favors instant food. However, there is nothing more special and creative than the work of a housewife who prepares food for her family. Despite the changing world and environment around us, housewives continue to concern themselves with their family's health and prepare delicious meals.

I am a pastor of an ethnic church in a multi-cultural society in which the majority of the congregation is first-generation immigrants. As I gather a variety of ingredients for the preparation of my weekly offering of spiritual food, I often refer to resources from all over the world. Every time I see appetizing meals, I recognize hearty tastes and the housewives' concerns for their families' health and happiness.

I met Ms. Jae Ok Chang through my ministry. She has dedicated herself as a housewife and cooking instructor for the benefit of her community with a clergy-like attitude. I am so pleased that she has written this bilingual cookbook full of recipes which are visually appealing as well as delicious and nutritional for Korean-Americans.

I gladly recommend this precious book to all Korean-Americans and our future generations.

Pastor David Kisuk Kang
The Korean Central Presbyterian Church of Cleveland

재미교포 **장재옥** 여사의 **30년 요리연구** !

A thirty-year study by Korean-American immigrant,
Ms.Jae-ok Chang

우리요리 이야기
Vignette of Korean Cooking

PART 1

육류요리 (Beef and meat dishes)

오렌지쇠고기요리 (Orange Beef)	12
쇠고기 탕수육 (Sweet and Sour Beef)	14
불고기 Ⅰ (Korean Barbeque Beef Ⅰ)	16

PART 1

육류요리 (Beef and meat dishes)

불고기 Ⅱ (Korean Barbeque Beef Ⅱ)	17
소·양 불고기 (Barbequed Tripe)	18
갈비찜 Ⅰ (Stewed Beef Ribs Ⅰ)	19
갈비찜 Ⅱ (Stewed Beef Ribs Ⅱ)	20
배즙갈비찜 (Stewed Beef Ribs with Pear Juice)	22
생강닭요리 (Ginger Chicken)	24
생강닭꼬치 (Ginger Chicken on Brochette)	26
닭볶음 (Chicken with Green Chilies)	27
닭고기 보쌈 (Lettuce Wrapped Chicken)	28

아구찜 (Braised Monk Fish)	44
생선탕수육 (Sweet and Sour Fish)	46
골뱅이 해초무침 (Conch and Fresh Kelp Salad)	48
해파리냉채 (Cold Jellyfish Salad)	50
오징어젓 (Pickled Squid)	52
오징어 장어구이 (Broiled Squid)	53
오징어 강정 (Fried Squid Dish)	54
오징어 야채무침 (Squid salad)	56
생굴 무침 (Oysters with Radish)	57
팔보채 (Eight Treasures Dish)	58
해삼탕 (Sea Cucumber Dish)	60

축하의 글 (Letters of congratulations)

이동성 (의학박사)
Ohio, Dong Sung Lee (M.D., Ph.D.,Ohio) — 6

오세근 (한인회장)
Se Keun Oh (President, The Korean American
Association of the greater Cleveland)

이재원 (클리블랜드 주립대 교수)
Jae Won Lee (Professor, Cleveland State University Cleveland, Ohio) — 7

구영환 (한인 중앙장로교회 원로목사)
John Young Hwan Koo, (Ph.D.Pastor-Emeritus, The Korean
Central Presbyterian Church of Cleveland)

Maria Schmidt (Director, Medical Imaging) — 8

이정은 (영양사)
Jane Lee Han (RD, LD Registered, L icensed and Consulting Dietitian)

강기석 (클리블랜드 중앙장로교회 담임목사)
David Ki Suk Kang (Pastor, The Korean Central
Presbyterian Church of Cleveland) — 9

굴을 곁들인 돼지보쌈 (Oyster and Pork Wrap)	30
돼지불고기 (Spicy Barbeque Pork)	32

PART 2

해물요리 (Seafood dishes)

해물순두부 (Seafood with Soft Bean Curd)	33
매운새우와 매운조갯살 (Spicy Shrimp and Scallops)	34
연어토막구이 (Pan-Fried Salmon)	36
크게 썬 무, 갈치조림 (Braised Ribbonfish with Radish)	38
꼬타리조림 (Braised Pollack)	39
홍어무침 (Spicy Raw Ray)	40
맛게살전, 게살꼬치 (Crab Cakes, Skewered Crabmeat)	41
황백생선전 (Pan Fried Yellow and White Fish Slices)	42

해물파전 (Pan Fried Spring Onion Patties with Seafood)	62
국수를 곁들인 낙지볶음 (Stir-Fried Octopus with Noodles)	64

PART 3

국수·국물요리류 (Noodle and Soups)

어묵, 야채, 우동전골 (Hot Pot with Fishcake, Vegetables and Noodles)	66
왕만두전골 (Stuffed Giant Dumplings)	68
오색소면전골 (Colorful Hot Pot with Noodles)	70
해물찌개 (Seafood Hot Pot)	71
김치찌개전골 (Kimchi Hot Pot)	72
미역국 (Seaweed Soup)	73
육개장 (Hearty Beef Soup)	74
갈비탕 (Beef Rib Soup)	75

대구매운탕 (Hot Spicy Cod Fish Casserole) 76

대구탕국 (Codfish Soup) 77

낙지, 버섯, 새우쌈요리 (Lettuce Wrapped Seafood) 78

뚝배기 된장찌개 (Traditional Bean Paste Dish) 80

떡국 (Rice Cake Soup) 81

만두국, 물만두국 (Stuffed Dumpling Soup, Boiled Dumplings) 82

해장국 (Hot and Spicy Soup) 84

북어국 (Dried Pollack Soup) 85

오색냉소면 (Five-Colors Cold Noodle) 86

자장면 (Noodles with Black Bean Sauce) 88

짬뽕 (Special Combination Noodle Soup) 89

풋고추장아찌 (Pickled Green Chilies) 100

무말랭이 오징어김치 (Dried Radish Kimchi with Dried Squid) 101

굴깍두기 (Radish Kimchi with Oysters) 102

썬김지 (Sliced Cabbage Kimchi) 103

오이소박이 (Stuffed Cucumber Kimchi) 104

동치미 (Mild Radish Kimchi) 105

백김지 (Mild Cabbage Kimchi) 106

보쌈김지 (Cabbage Leaf Wrapped Kimchi) 107

나박김지 (Light Kimchi) 108

팔색 미역냉채나물 (Colorful Seaweed Salad) 122

오색모듬말이 (Five Color Rolls) 124

겨자채 (Seafood Salad with Mustard Dressing) 126

잡채 (Transparent Noodles with Vegetables) 128

양장피잡채 (Salad with Mungbean Starch Sheet) 130

두부명란젓찜 (Bean Curd with Fish Roe) 132

두부고추장 볶음 (Spicy Bean Curd) 133

두부구이 (Pan-Fried Bean Curd) 134

어묵떡볶이 (Fried Fishcake with Rice Cake) 135

떡볶이 (Stir-Fried Rice Cake) 136

꽃게장담그기 (Pickled Crab) 138

PART 5
밥 류 (Rice dishes)

계절별 요리
(Season dishes)

봄 (Spring) 148

여름 (Summer) 149

가을 (Fall) 150

겨울 (Winter) 151

비빔냉면 (Buckwheat Noodles) 90

물냉면 (Buckwheat Noodle Soup) 91

콩국 (Creamy Soy Bean Soup) 92

소면장국수 (Thin Noodle Soup with Spicy Sauce) 93

PART 4
김치, 마른반찬류
(Kimchi and side dishes)

같은 소스로 10가지 이상
마른반찬 만들기 (Basic Sauce for Side Dishes) 94

더덕구이 (Spicy Codoropsis Root) 96

그린빈요리 (Seasoned Green Beans) 97

우엉조림 (Burdock Root Cho-rim) 98

콩조림 (Black Beans in Soy Sauce) 99

카레라이스 (Rice with Curry Sauce) 109

비빔밥 (Rice with Vegetables) 110

회덮밥 (Rice Topped with Raw Fish) 112

볶음밥 (Fried Rice) 113

김밥소개 (Sushi) 114

막기김밥 (Rolled Sushi) 115

꽃다발, 야채김밥이미지 (California , Vegetable Roll Image) 116

꽃다발, 야채김밥 (California , Vegetable Roll) 117

보쌈김밥 (Do It Yourself Sushi) 118

모듬초밥 (Assorted Seafood Sushi) 120

PART 6
별미요리 (Specials)

약식 (Steamed Sweet Rice) 139

마이크로 오븐찰떡 (Microwave Rice Cakes) 140

오복경단떡 (Sweet Rice Dumplings) 141

구절판 (Korean Hord' oeuvres) 142

꼰만두 구이 (Pan-fried Dumplings) 143

팥죽 (Red Bean Soup with Dumplings) 144

잣죽 (Creamy Pine Nut Soup) 145

수정과 (Ginger Flavored Persimmon Dessert) 146

귤 · 배 · 생강차 (Ginger Tea with Pear and Orange) 147

육·류·고·기·요·리 (Beef and meat dishes)

오렌지쇠고기요리 (Orange Beef)

🍳 준비는 이렇게(5인분)

쇠고기 1½ lbs, 오렌지즙 ¼ 컵, 생강 2쪽(잘게 다짐), 계란 흰자 1개, 베이킹소다 1작은술, 밀가루 3큰술 + 녹말가루 3큰술, 생강물 ½ 컵, 후추 약간(½작은술), 식용유 1큰술, 채썬 오렌지껍질 20개 정도, 흰깨, 잣 약간, 식용유 4컵

🍳 만드는 것은 이렇게

❶ 쇠고기를 먹기좋은 크기로(가로 1인치, 세로 2½인치 정도) 얇게 썰어 밀가루에 묻힌 후 (식용유 1큰술, 채썬 오렌지껍질 20개 정도, 흰깨, 잣 약간, 식용유 4컵)을 제외한 위의 재료들을 잘 혼합하여 1시간 정도 냉장고에 넣어 두었다가 식용유 4컵의 기름에 2번 튀겨낸다.

❷ 프라이팬에 식용유 1큰술을 두르고 만들어 놓은 소스를 5큰술 넣고 보글보글할 때 튀겨놓은 고기를 두 번에 나누어 소스와 같이 볶아낸다.(1~2분 정도)

❸ 접시에 내놓기 전에 채썬 오렌지껍질, 흰깨, 잣을 뿌린다

🍳 소스 준비는 이렇게

생강물 ¼ 컵, 마늘 2쪽(납작하게 썬다), 오렌지 ½(4쪽으로 썬다), 간장 ⅓ cup (6큰술), 브라운설탕 1 cup, 물엿 1컵, 포도주 2큰술, 참기름 1큰술

🍳 소스 만드는 것은 이렇게

판판한 냄비에 소스 재료들을 분량대로 넣고 센불에 12분 정도 거품이 날때까지 조린다. (마늘 2쪽과 오렌지 4쪽은 버린다.)

✽ 매운 것을 원할 때는 마른 붉은 고추를 소스 볶을 때 같이 넣으면 맛이 일품이다.

✽ 소스는 냉동에 보관하면 오랫동안 간직할 수 있다.

✽ Sweet & Sour Sauce는 중국제품(LACHOY 東)임.

🍳 5 servings

1½ lbs. beef, cut bite sized, 3 tbsp. flour, 3 tbsp. cornstarch, ¼ cup orange juice, 2 slices ginger, minced, 1 egg white, 1 tsp. baking soda, 1 tbsp oil, ½ cup ginger water, ½ tsp. black pepper, 4 cups oil for frying , 20 pieces orange rind

🍳 Making

Dredge the beef in a flour and cornstarch mixture. Gently mix in a combination of orange juice, ginger, egg white, baking soda, pepper and ginger water. Refrigerate for 1 hour.

Combine all the sauce ingredients, except the orange rind, sesame seeds and pine nuts, and boil on high heat for about 12 minutes until thickened and bubbly on top. Fry the beef pieces in small batches, placing them in hot oil one by one to prevent them from sticking together. For crispness, fry each piece twice.

To serve, heat 1 tablespoon of cooking oil in a skillet and add 5 tablespoons of sauce, saving the rest for later use. Add the beef, coat well (this may be done in two batches for a more even coating) and immediately serve. Garnish the dish with orange rind, sesame seeds and pine nuts.

🍳 For the sauce

¼ cup ginger water, 2 cloves garlic, ½ orange, 6 tbsp. soy sauce, 1 cup brown sugar, 1 cup corn syrup, 2 tbsp.wine, 1 tbsp. sesame oil, 1 tbsp. cooking oil, 1 orange rind, cut in strips, 1 tbsp. sesame seeds, pine nuts for garnish

✽ Note : The sauce stores well in the freezer for many months.
For a spicier sauce, add some dried red chilies.

✽ Sweet & Sour Sauce is available in Asian groceries (LACHOY 東)

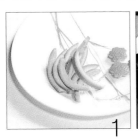    

1 2 3 4 5

육 · 류 · 고 · 기 · 요 · 리 (Beef and meat dishes)

쇠고기탕수육 (Sweet and Sour Beef)

준비는 이렇게 (4인분)

쇠고기 ⅔ lb, 녹말가루 1컵, 베이킹소다 ½작은술, 달걀흰자 1개, 물 1컵, 당근(중간크기) 1개, 파(흰뿌리만) 4쪽, 잣 ½큰술, 배춧잎 1장, 목이버섯 ½컵, 식용유 3컵

만드는 것은 이렇게

❶ 먼저 쇠고기를 먹기 좋은 크기(손가락 두 번째마디)로 썰어 녹말가루 ½컵에 베이킹소다 ½작은술 넣고 잘 주물러둔다.
❷ 녹말가루 ½컵에 흰자 1개, 물1컵을 부어 섞은후 ❶의 고기를 넣고 혼합하여 끓는 식용유에 2번 튀겨낸다.

소스 준비는 이렇게

생강 20쪽(납작썰음), 소금 ½작은술, 물 2컵, Sweet & Sour Sauce 3½큰술, 파인애플통조림국물 10oz(½컵), 흑설탕 1½큰술, 식초 ½작은술, 녹말가루 1½큰술(물 3큰술에 풀어둠), 화학조미료 ¼작은술(식성에 따라 첨가할 수도 있음)

소스 만드는 것은 이렇게

❶ 생강 20쪽을 물2컵을 붓고 매운 냄새가 날 때까지 끓여둔다. (10분정도) 생강은 버린다.
❷ 끓인 생강물에 Sweet & Sour Sauce 3½큰술, 소금 ½작은술, 파인애플통조림 국물 10oz, 흑설탕 1½큰술, 식초 ½작은술을 넣고 끓이다가 물에 탄 녹말가루(녹말가루1큰술, 물 3큰술)를 넣어 걸쭉하게 되면 불을 끈다.
❸ 여러 가지 모양(꽃모양, 톱니모양 등)의 당근과 파(어슷어슷 썰음), 배추줄기(길게 썰음-6피스), 목이버섯(물에 불려 잘 씻은)을 소스에 넣는다. 프라이팬에 모든 소스와 튀긴 고기를 같이 넣고 잘 혼합한뒤 판판한 접시에 담아낸다. 잣도 뿌린다.

∗물에 탄 녹말가루를 사용할 경우 물과 녹말가루를 타놓고 앙금이 가라앉으면 위의 물은 버리고 앙금만 쓰면 더욱 바삭바삭하다.
∗ Sweet & Sour Sauce는 중국제품(LACHOY 東)임.
∗식성에 따라 설탕이나 식초등 더 첨가해도 됨.

4 servings

⅔ lb. beef, cut in bite size pieces, 1 cup cornstarch, ½ tsp.baking soda, 1 egg white , 1 cup water to make batter, 3 cups cooking oil for frying, 1medium carrot, sliced or cut in flower shapes, 4 spring onions, white parts only, cut diagonally in 2″pieces, 1Napa cabbage leaf, stalk only, cut in 6 long bite sized strips, pine nuts for garnish

Making

Dredge the beef in a mixture of ½ cup cornstarch and the baking soda. To make a batter, combine ½ cup cornstarch with the egg white and 1 cup water.
Coat the beef pieces in the batter and fry in hot oil. For crispness, fry the beef twice.

For sweet and sour sauce

20 slices ginger, 3½ tbsp. prepared sweet and sour sauce∗, 2 cups water, ½ tsp. vinegar, ½ cup pineapple juice, ½ tsp. salt, 1½ tbsp. brown sugar, 1½ tbsp. cornstarch mixed with 3 tbsp. water

Sauce Making

Boil water with the ginger until a strong ginger aroma emerges, about 10 minutes.
Discard the ginger, add the remaining sauce ingredients, except the cornstarch mixed with water, and heat. Thicken with the cornstarch mixed with water.
Add the carrot slices, spring onions and cabbage strips. Place the fried beef on a serving platter and pour the sauce over it. Serve at once with pine nuts for garnish.

∗ Note : The amount of sugar and vinegar can be adjusted to taste.
∗ Sweet & Sour Sauce is available in Asian groceries (LACHOY 東)

1　2　3　4

불고기 I (Korean Barbeque Beef I, Boul-Koh-Kee)

🥢 준비는 이렇게(5인분)

쇠고기 2½lbs., 물 1큰술, 포도주 1½큰술, 후추 ½작은술, 참기름 ⅓컵, Sprite ⅓컵, 흑설탕 ½컵, 진간장 ⅓컵

🥢 만드는 것은 이렇게

쇠고기(Spencer Roast) 2½lbs.를 아주 얇게(스끼야끼 스타일로) 썰어 판판한 그릇에 담고 물과 설탕을 넣고 잘 주무르다가 준비한 재료를 분량대로 다 혼합하여 잘 버무린 다음 프라이팬에 굽거나 오븐에 브로일로 굽든지 석쇠에 구워도 된다.

🥢 5 servings

2½ lbs. beef (Spencer roast or similar), thinly sliced, 1 tbsp. water, ½ cup brown sugar, ½ tsp. black pepper, 1½ tbsp. cooking wine, ⅓ cup sesame oil, ⅓ cup soy sauce, ⅓ cup Sprite (carbonated lemon beverage)

🥢 *Making*

Add water and sugar to beef and mix very gently by hand. Combine the remaining ingredients and again mix gently with the beef. To cook, barbeque on a grill, broil or sizzle in a hot preheated, ungreased skillet.

육 · 류 · 고 · 기 · 요 · 리 (Beef and meat dishes)

불고기 II (Korean Barbeque Beef II , Boul-Koh-Kee)

🍴 준비는 이렇게(5인분)

쇠고기 2½lbs., 포도주 3큰술, 후추 ½작은술, 참기름 ⅓컵, 중간 크기양파 ½개, 흑설탕 2½큰술, 진간장 ⅓컵, 다진마늘 1큰술, 잣가 루 1½큰술

🍴 만드는 것은 이렇게

❶ 쇠고기(Spencer Roast) 2½lbs.를 아주 얇게(스키야키 스 타일로) 썰어 놓고 양파는 강판에 가루가 되게 갈아놓는다.

❷ 잣 1½큰술을 칼로 잘게 다져놓고 마늘 4개를 다져 1큰술되 게 준비한다.

❸ 양념재료가 다 준비되면 넓고 판판한 그릇에 얇게 썬 고기를 담고 양념재료들을 넣어 잘 버물어 놓은 후 프라이팬에 굽던 지 오븐 브로일, 또는 불고기 굽는 석쇠에 굽는다.

🍴 5 servings

2½ lbs. beef (Spencer roast or similar), thinly sliced, 3 tbsp. wine, ½ tsp. black pepper, ⅓ cup sesame oil, ½ medium onion grated, 2½ tbsp. brown sugar, ⅓ cup soy sauce, 1 tbsp. minced garlic, 1½ tbsp. pine nuts, crushed

🍴 Making

Combine all the ingredients, except the beef, and then rub the mixture very gently into the beef.

To cook, barbeque on a grill, broil or sear (sizzle) in a hot, ungreased skillet.

㉭·류·고·기·요·리 (Beef and meat dishes)

소·양 불고기(Barbequed Tripe)

🥘 준비는 이렇게(6인분)

소양 3 lbs., (손바닥 반 정도의 크기로 14 piece 정도), 마늘 5쪽, 소금 3큰술, 생강 다진것 1작은술, 볶음 고추장 2½큰술, 참기름 3큰술, 후추 ½작은술, Cooking Wine 큰술, 흑설탕 2큰술, 간장 1½큰술, 물 4컵

🥘 만드는 것은 이렇게

❶ 소·양은 먼저 기름을 골고루 잘라내고 소금(3큰술) 정도 넣고 바락바락 주물러 미지근한 물에 2, 3번 반복 씻어낸다.

❷ 물 4컵 정도 넣고 젓가락으로 찔러 연하게 들어갈 때까지 끓인 다음 다시 깨끗이 씻어내고 모든 재료를 넣고 골고루 주물러 놓은 뒤 한 시간쯤 간이 잘 밴 뒤에 불에 굽는다.

❸ 먹기 좋은 크기로 썰어 접시에 담아 낸다.

🥘 6 servings

3 lbs. tripe, trimmed of fat, cut 3″ squares (about 14 pieces) , 3 tbsp. salt, 5 cloves garlic, 1 tsp. ginger, minced, 2½ tbsp. seasoned hot chili paste*, 3 tbsp. sesame oil, ½ tsp. black pepper, 1 tbsp. cooking wine, 2 tbsp. brown sugar, 1½ tbsp. soy sauce, 4 cups water

🥘 Making

Thoroughly rub tripe with the salt. Rinse well in warm water.
In a saucepan, add tripe and enough water, about 4 cups, to cover and cook until tender when tested with a fork. Rinse it once again. Combine the remaining ingredients, mix into tripe and let stand for an hour.
Grill tripe on a charcoal fire or broil. Cut into bite sized pieces and serve.

* Available in Asian groceries and super market.

갈비찜 | (Stewed Beef Ribs Ⅰ, Kal-bi Chim)

🍲 준비는 이렇게(8~10인분)

갈비 5 lbs., 무(중간크기) ⅓, 밤 15개, 대추 10개, 은행 20개, 계란 1개, 버섯 5개, 간장 ¾컵, 설탕 ½컵, 참기름 3큰술, 후추 1작은술, 파 3뿌리, 마늘 4쪽, 양파 1개, 실고추 약간, 잣 약간

🍲 만드는 것은 이렇게

❶ 갈비는 굵직하게 칼집을 내고 냄비에 담아 고기가 잠기게 물을 붓고 끓인다.

❷ 끓으면 핏물과 기름기를 씻어내고 간장과 물을 고기가 잠길 정도로 부어 20분 정도 센불에 끓인 다음, 불을 중간불로 낮춘다. 무와 당근(큼직하게 썬 것), 밤, 버섯, 양파, 양념을 넣어 뭉근하게 한시간 정도 끓이고 거의 다 되었을 때 씨를 뺀 대추를 넣는다.

❸ 은행을 파랗게 볶는다.(프라이팬에)

❹ 갈비를 그릇에 담고 황백지단과 은행을 얹는다. 실고추와 잣도 뿌린다.
(주의할 것은 갈비를 끓일 때 자주 물을 넣지 말 것)

🍲 8~10 servings

5 lbs. beef ribs, cut 1½″ long, ¾ cup soy sauce, ½ lb. small radish, cut in 4 pieces, 15 chestnuts, shelled and blanched, 5 dried black mushrooms, softened in warm water, cut in halves, 1 carrot cut in, 5 pieces, 1 medium onion, 3 spring onions, ½ cup sugar, 3 tbsp. sesame oil, 1 tsp. black pepper, 4 cloves garlic, minced, 10 dried red dates, pitted, 20 ginkgo nuts, fine nuts, fried egg pancake strips for garnish

🍲 Making

Trim fat from ribs. Put ribs in a large pot with enough water to cover and boil for 5-6 minutes. Discard the water and rinse ribs thoroughly. Return ribs to the cleaned pot, add enough water to cover and the soy sauce and cook for 20 minutes on high heat. Reduce heat and add the radish, corrot, chestnuts, mushrooms, onion, whole spring onions, sugar, sesame oil, black pepper and garlic. Simmer for an hour.
Add the red dates and continue simmering for a few more minutes.
To serve, garnish with toasted ginkgo nuts and fried egg strips.

✻ Note : When boiling the ribs, try to avoid adding any additional
water.

갈비찜II(Stewed Beef Ribs II, Kal-bi Chim)

🍲 준비는 이렇게(20~30인분)

갈비 20 lbs., 물, 감초뿌리 15조각

🍲 소스 준비는 이렇게

진간장 2½ 컵, 참기름 1½ 컵, 흑설탕 2½ 컵, 물엿 ½ 컵, 포도주 ⅔ 컵, 마늘즙 1½ 큰술, 생강즙 1큰술, 후추 1½ 작은술

＊소스 재료들을 분량대로 넣고 잘 섞어 준비함

🍲 갈비 삶기

❶ 갈비는 기름이 깊이 배어 있으므로 토막을 내면서(뼈를 중심으로 고깃살이 양쪽으로 2½ 인치 세로, 1.8 인치 가로 정도)기름을 완전히 잘라낸 뒤 판판한 큰 솥에 갈비 (20 lbs.)가 잠길 정도로 물을 붓고 한번 헹군 뒤, 갈비에 다시 잠길 정도의 물을 붓고 끓으면 그 물을 버린다.(핏물제거)

❷ 다시 한번 새 물을 갈비에 잠길 정도로 붓고 감초뿌리(1.8인치 세로, 0.6인치 가로)(15조각)를 넣고 푹 삶는다. (소요시간: 1시간10분~1시간20분) 감초뿌리는 버린다.

❸ 푹 삶아진 갈비고기와 국물을 완전히 분리, 갈비고기만 판판한 크고 두꺼운 뚜껑있는 프라이팬(사방 12인치,깊이 3인치 정도)이나 다른 냄비도 같은 사이즈 정도면 된다. (밑이 두꺼울수록 타지 않음)

❹ 위의 만들어놓은 소스를 먼저 프라이팬에 2컵 넣고 삶은 갈비고기 35~40 PCs. 정도를 냄비에 소스와 같이 넣고 뚜껑을 덮고 2분쯤 있으면 보글보글 거품이 난다. 이때 갈비를 사방 가장자리로 밀고 중간에 주걱이 들어갈 정도로 비우면 소스가 몰려중앙에서 보글보글할 때 주걱으로 고기위에 끼얹는다.

❺ 11분 정도 되면 소스가 자작자작하며 고기가 진한 브라운색으로 변하고 반짝반짝한다. 고기를 너무 뒤적거리거나 무리하게 다루면 뼈가 빠진다.

❻ 갈비찜으로 손색이 없으려면 고기가 연하면서 풀리지 않고 뼈가 붙어 있어야 됨. 3번정도(20lbs.) 같은 방법으로 볶으면 된다. 상에 낼 때 잣만 뿌린다.

＊미국에서는 파트럭 디너 같은 파티가 자주 있다. 모이는 사람들이 메뉴를 짜서 각자 한가지(요리접시)씩 해서 모인다. 그때 주인집에서 준비하는 것은 대개 불고기나 갈비찜,김치, 드링크, 과일 정도로 준비할 때 위의 갈비찜을 하면 좋다. 미리 2, 3일전에 준비할 수도 있고 또 2, 3주전에 해서 냉동했다가 다시 끓이면 그대로 금방 한 것 같이 좋다.

＊집을 떠난 자녀들이 크리스마스 때나 추수감사절 때쯤 오게 되면 사람이 많이 모이므로 미리해서 냉동에 두었다가 명절에 다시 데우기만 하면 되니까 일손을 훨씬 덜 수 있다.

＊갈비를 냉동해 두었다가 다시 조리할 때는 물을 솥 밑바닥에 약간 붓고 중간 불에서 데우는 것이 좋다.

＊갈비 삶은 육수를 냉장고에 넣어 하루나 이틀 뒤에 기름이 하얗게 뜨면 완전히 걷고 육수국물로 어디든지 쓰면 진국이다.

＊소스도 남을 경우 냉동에 보관 오랫동안 두고 써도 무방함.

＊감초뿌리는 동양식품에서 구입할 수 있다.

🍲 20~30 servings

20 lbs. beef ribs, cut in 2½″ long pieces, 15 slices licorice root＊, 2½ cups dark soy sauce, 1½ cups sesame oil, 2½ cups brown sugar, ½ cup corn syrup, ⅔ cup wine, 1 tbsp. garlic juice, 1 tbsp. ginger juice, 1 ½ tsp. black pepper, pine nuts for garnish

🍲 Making

Trim the fat and place the ribs in a large stock pot. Add enough water to cover and boil for 3 minutes. Discard the water, rinse the pot and ribs thoroughly in warm running water, removing all the residue.

Return the ribs to the pot, add the licorice slices and enough water to cover again, bring to a boil, reduce the heat and simmer for 1-1½ hours until the meat is tender but still clings to the bones.

Discard the licorice, remove the meat and reserve the stock for later use. Prepare a marinade sauce by mixing all the remaining ingredients, except the pine nuts.

In a heavy skillet, place one layer of ribs (may need to cook them in several batches) and pour in 2 cups of the marinade sauce. Cover the skillet and boil on medium heat for 2 minutes, until bubbly. Use a spoon to baste the ribs 2-3 times with sauce from the bottom of the skillet.

Continue cooking for 10-12 minutes, until the sauce gets very thick and starts to sizzle. The ribs should be a dark, rich, shiny color.

Handle the ribs gently to keep the meat from falling off the bones. Garnish with pine nuts.

＊ Note : This dish can be prepared 2-3 days ahead and can be frozen 2-3 weeks. To reheat and prevent burning, add a little water to a skillet and use medium heat.
Stock can easily be skimmed by refrigerating it until the fat solidifies and, once skimmed, it will be a good base for soup.

＊ Available in Asian groceries.

육·류·고·기·요·리 (Beef and meat dishes)

배즙갈비찜 (Stewed Beef Ribs with Pear Juice)

🍲 준비는 이렇게(8~10인분)

갈비 5 lbs., 배(중간배 3개, 한국배 큰 것 1½) (작은 것은 4개 정도), 중간크기 당근 1개, 진간장 ¾컵, 후추 1작은술, 참기름 ½컵, 대추 30 개, 밤 20 개. 마늘즙 2큰술, 생강즙 1큰술, 포도주 2큰술, 정종 2큰술, 육수 4컵, 감초뿌리 7조각

🍲 만드는 것은 이렇게

❶ 갈비고기에는 기름이 많이 배어 있으므로 토막을 내면서 (뼈를 중심으로 고깃살이 양쪽으로 6cm 세로, 4cm가로 정도)기름을 부분으로 잘라낸 다음 미지근한 물에 한번 헹군다.

❷ 갈비에 물이 잠길 정도로 냄비에 물을 붓고 끓이다가 끓으면 불을 끄고 그 국물을 다 버린다. (핏물임)

❸ 다시 한번 더 갈비고기에 잠길 정도로 물을 붓고 감초뿌리(4cm세로, 1cm가로) 7조각을 고기와 같이 넣고 끓으면서부터 10분 지난 뒤에 그 냄비 그대로 냉장고에 넣고 하룻밤을 지나고나서 하얗게 떠있는 기름을 깨끗이 걷어내고 감초뿌리도 버린 다음 갈비 고기와 육수를 분리한다.

🍲 갈비 소스는 이렇게

❶ 배와 당근, 마늘, 생강은 위의 분량대로 믹서기에 육수 1컵을 붓고 갈아 놓는다.(즙이 됨)

❷ 대추는 물에 불려 잘 씻어놓는다.

❸ 통조림의 밤(20개 정도)도 물기를 빼고 준비한다.

🍲 갈비찜은 이렇게

❶ 육수와 따로 분리해놓은 갈비에 배즙과 당근, 마늘, 생강즙을 붓고 35분 동안 끓인다.

❷ 양념(간장 ¾ 컵, 후추 1작은술, 참기름 ⅓ 컵, 대추 30개)을 같이 넣고 끓인다.

❸ 육수국물 3cup에 포도주 2큰술, 정종 2큰술, 밤 20개, 참기름 2 큰술 넣고 10분간 끓인 후에 끓인 국물을 위의 양념하여 조린 갈비에 붓고 중간불로 낮추고 끓고부터 20분 조린다.

　상에 낼 때 황백지단과 실고추, 실백과 은행볶음을 고명으로 쓴다.

＊ 대추, 감초뿌리는 동양식품점에서 구입

🍲 8~10 servings

5 lbs. beef ribs, cut 1½″ long, 7 slices licorice root*, 3-4 pears (Anjou or large Asian pear), cored, 1 medium carrot, cut in small pieces, 30 dried, pitted red dates*, rinsed, 20 chestnuts, shelled and blanched, 2 tbsp. garlic juice, 1 tbsp. ginger juice, 2 tbsp. rice wine, 2 tbsp. wine, ½ cup sesame oil, 1 tsp. black pepper, ¾ cup dark soy sauce, 4 cups stock, see recipe

＊ garnishes : fried egg strips, shredded red chili and toasted ginkgo nuts

🍲 Making

Trim the fat and rinse the ribs thoroughly in warm running water. Place ribs in a large pot, add enough water to cover and boil for 5-6 minutes. Discard the water and rinse the ribs. Return ribs to a clean pot with enough water to cover, add the licorice slices and boil for 10 minutes. Remove the pot from the heat, cool and refrigerate overnight or until the fat solidifies.

The next day, skim the solidified fat and discard the licorice slices. Heat the stock until it liquefies. Remove the ribs, reserving the stock.

In a food processor, puree the pears, carrot, garlic and ginger with 1 cup of the stock. Add this mix to ribs in a heavy pot and cook 35 minutes. Add 2 tablespoons sesame oil, black pepper, dates and soy sauce and set aside. In a sauce pan, add 3 cups of stock, the rice wine, cooking wine, 2 tables poons sesame oil and the chestnuts and boil for 10 minutes. Add this mixture to the pot with the ribs, reduce heat and simmer 20 minutes over medium heat. To serve, garnish with fried egg strips, shredded red chili and toasted ginkgo nuts.

＊ Available in Asian groceries.

육 · 류 · 고 · 기 · 요 · 리 (Beef and meat dishes)

생강닭요리 (Ginger Chicken)

🥘 준비는 이렇게(10인분)

닭 2½ lbs.

🥘 소스 준비는 이렇게

물 1½ 컵, 생강 10쪽, 간장 ⅔ 컵, 참기름 1큰술, 브라운 설탕 2 컵,
Sweet & Sour Sauce 3큰술
* 잘 혼합하여 끓이다가 끓고부터 20분 졸임. (생강 10쪽은 버린다.)
* Sweet & Sour Sauce는 중국제품(LACHOY 東)임.

🥘 닭고기 반죽은 이렇게

마늘 1쪽(다진 것), 생강 다진것 1작은술, 포도주 1작은술, 후추 ¼, 베
이킹소다 1작은술, 베이킹파우더 ½작은술, 밀가루 ½ 컵, 녹말 1½ 컵,
물 ⅔ 컵, 식용유 4컵
* 기름없는 가슴흰살부위 닭고기의 껍질을 벗기고 깨끗이 씻은 후에
먹기 좋은 크기로 (가로1인치,세로1.5인치) 썰어 닭고기반죽에 잘 혼합
하여 20~30분 정도 냉장고에 넣었다가 뜨거운 식용유에 갈색이 나도록
2번 튀긴다.

🥘 만드는 것은 이렇게

❶ 위에 소스를 넣기 전에 프라이팬에 식용유 3큰술을 넣고 소
스 ⅔ 컵 넣고 보글보글 끓으면 튀겨놓은 닭고기를 두 번
나누어 넣어 흔들면서 불 조절한다.
❷ 잘 혼합, 2분 정도 조린다. 잣가루와 흰 깨를 위에 뿌린다.

🥘 10 servings

2½ lbs. boneless and skinless chicken, cut bite-sized, 1 clove garlic,
minced finely (about 1 teaspoon), 2 slices ginger, minced (about 1
teaspoon), 1 tsp. wine, dash black pepper, ½ cup flour, ½ tsp.
baking soda, 1½ cup cornstarch, ⅔ cup water, 4 cup oil for frying
* garnishes : sesame seeds and crushed pine nuts

🥘 For ginger sauce

1½ cups water, 10 slices ginger, ⅔ cup soy sauce, 1 tbsp. sesame
oil, 2 cups brown sugar, 3 tbsp. prepared sweet and sour sauce
* Bring all to boil and thickened for additional 20 minutes, Discard
ginger slices.
* Sweet & Sour Sauce is available in Asian groceries (LACHOY 東)

🥘 Making

Combine all the ginger sauce ingredients in a pan and boil for 20
minutes on medium high heat. Discard the ginger. (Sauce can be stored
in the freezer for up to a year.) In a bowl, combine the chicken and the
rest of the ingredients, except the oil and garnishes, and refrigerate for
20-30 minutes. Then fry the chicken in small batches, placing pieces
one by one in the hot oil to preven them from sticking together. For
crispness, fry the chicken twice. Keep warm in the oven.When ready
to serve, heat 3 tablespoons of oil in a skillet and add ⅔ cup of ginger
sauce, saving the rest for later use.
Add the fried chicken, coat with the sauce and cook for 2 minutes.
Serve immediately. Garnish with sesame seeds and crushed pine nuts
to taste.

육·류·고·기·요·리 (Beef and meat dishes)

생강닭꼬치(Ginger Chicken on Brochette)

🥢 준비는 이렇게(10인분)

닭 2½ lbs.

🥢 소스 준비는 이렇게

물 1½ 컵, 생강 10쪽, 간장 ⅔ 컵, 참기름 1큰술, 브라운설탕 2 컵, Sweet & Sour Sauce 3큰술

＊ 잘 혼합하여 끓이다가 끓고부터 20분 졸임.

🥢 만드는 것은 이렇게

❶ 생강 닭요리와 같은 소스를 만들고, 닭을 먹기 좋은 크기로(사방 1인치) 썰어 소스를 묻혀서 꼬치에 끼우고 오븐에 브로일로 구워낸다.

❷ 3개씩 꼬치에 5조각으로 12분 브로일함. (6분쯤 뒤에 소스를 한번 더 바르면 윤기가 남)

＊ 소스는 생강 닭요리 소스와 같다.

🥢 10 servings

2½ lbs. boneless and skinless chicken, cut in 1″ cubes, 15 pieces, ⅔-1 cup ginger sauce (use recipe from Ginger Chicken), 3 to 5 bamboo sticks (soaked in water) or metal skewers

🥢 Making

Gently toss the chicken in the ginger sauce. Skewer 3 or 5 pieces on sticks. Broil under oven broiler or barbeque on hibachi for about 12 minutes.

Turn frequently to cook thoroughly and brush with sauce to give the chicken a richer appearance.

육 · 류 · 고 · 기 · 요 · 리 (Beef and meat dishes)

닭볶음(Chicken with Green Chilies)

🦪 준비는 이렇게(5인분)

닭 1 lbs., 간장 2큰술, 마늘 3쪽, 풋고추 10개, 설탕 1½ 큰술, 쿠킹와인 2큰술, 소금, 후추 ¼작은술, 참기름 2큰술, 실고추 1작은술

🦪 만드는 것은 이렇게

❶ 닭을 먹기좋은 크기로 토막냄. 소금과 후추를 조금씩 뿌리고 쿠킹와인을 붓고 30분정도 둠.

❷ 프라이팬에 참기름을 분량대로 붓고 마늘을 잘 다져넣은 후 센 불에 토막친 닭을 넣고 약간 탈 정도로 볶음.

❸ 풋고추를 길쭉길쭉하게 썰어놓고 볶은 닭 위에 간장과 설탕을 넣고 조린 후 풋고추와 실고추를 넣은 후 약한 불에 익힌다.

＊마늘을 사용해도 전혀 마늘냄새가 나지 않는 것이 특징.

🦪 5 servings

1 lbs. chicken, cut into bite-size pieces, ¼ tsp. salt, ¼ tsp. black pepper, 2 tbsp. cooking wine, 2 tbsp. sesame oil, 3 cloves garlic, minced, 10 green chilies cut into bite-size pieces, 2 tbsp. soy sauce, 1½ tbsp. sugar, 1 tsp. red chili, dried and shredded*

🦪 Making

Season the chicken with salt, pepper and the cooking wine and let stand for 30 minutes.

In a heavy skillet, heat the sesame oil, stir-fry the garlic first and then add the chicken pieces, browning over high heat almost to the burning point.

Add green chilies, soy sauce, sugar and, when no liquid remains, add the shredded red chili. Turn heat to low and cook until done.

＊ Note: Garlic enhances the flavor of this dish without making one's breath offensive.

＊Available in Asian groceries.

닭고기 보쌈(Lettuce Wrapped Chicken)

🍲 준비는 이렇게(5인분)

닭고기 1Pound, 간장 3큰술, 녹말가루 1큰술, 설탕 1큰술, 다진생강 ½ 큰술, 소금 ½작은술, 식용유 3큰술, 양상추잎 15개, 다진마늘 ½큰술, 양파(중간크기) 1개, 죽순 1oz(can)-잘게썰어 ⅓컵, 불린표고버섯 3장 .

🍲 만드는 것은 이렇게

❶ 닭고기는 가슴살이나 안심부위의 기름없는 것으로 기름을 완전히 발라낸다.

❷ 껍질도 완전히 벗긴 다음 완두콩 크기로 아주 잘게 깍둑썰기로 썰어놓는다.

❸ 썰어놓은 닭고기에 다진생강, 다진마늘, 진간장, 설탕, 소금, 녹말가루를 분량대로 넣고 30~40분 정도 냉장고에 넣어둔다.

❹ 양파와 죽순도 완두콩 모양으로 아주 잘게 썰고 표고버섯도 잘게 썰어둔다.

❺ 오목하고 판판한 프라이팬에 식용유 2큰술을 넣고 센불에 달구어질 때 닭고기를 넣어 부드럽게 익을 때까지 볶는다.

❻ 양파와 죽순, 표고버섯도 분량대로 준비된 것을 식용유 1큰술 넣고 볶다가 다시 닭고기를 넣어 함께 볶다가 프라이팬 가장자리에 양념장 섞은 것을 넣고 맛을 낸다.

❼ 준비한 양상치 15개를 깨끗이 씻어 물기를 없애고 찢어지지 않게 떼어 만들어놓은 닭요리를 각각 상치잎에 담아 상에 낸다. 만들어 놓은 자장소스에 찍어 먹는다.

＊당면을 튀겨서 접시 밑에 깔기도 하고 쑥갓을 깔기도 한다. 쑥갓을 쓸때는 방울 토마토를 몇 개, 모양으로 쓴다.

🍲 양념간장은 이렇게

진간장 2큰술, 정종 1½큰술, 참기름 1작은술, 후추가루 ½작은술

🍲 자장소스는 이렇게

자장 2큰술, 꿀 1큰술, 흑설탕 ½큰술, 물엿 ½큰술
＊재료를 다 함께 섞어 둔다.

🍲 5 servings

1Pound chicken breast, skinless and boneless, cut in pea size pieces,1 ½tsp. grated ginger, ½ tbsp. minced garlic, 3 tbsp. soy sauce, 1 tbsp. sugar, ½ tsp. salt, 1 tbsp. corn starch, 3 tbsp. cooking oil for frying, 1 medium onion, diced in pea sizes, ⅓ cup bamboo shoots, diced in pea sizes, 3 black mushroom, soften in water, diced, 15 lettuce leaves

🍲 Making

In a bowl, combine the chicken with the ginger, garlic, soy sauce, sugar, salt, egg yolk and cornstarch and refrigerate 30-40 minutes.

Make the seasoned soy sauce by combining its listed ingredients. Prepare the black bean dipping sauce by combining its ingredients and reserve in appropriate serving bowls.

In a skillet, heat the 2 tbsp. cooking oil and fry the chicken until done. Use a slotted spoon to transfer the chicken quickly to a plate. Pour off most of the oil, leaving 1 tablespoon in the skillet, and saute the black mushroom, onion and bamboo shoots. Add the chicken with the seasoned soy sauce.

Arrange the lettuce leaves on a serving platter. Serve so each diner can wrap some of the seasoned chicken in a lettuce leaf and dip it in black bean sauce.

🍲 For seasoned soy sauce

1 tbsp. soy sauce, 1½ tbsp. rice wine, 1 tsp. sesame oil, ½ tsp. black pepper

🍲 For black bean dipping sauce

2 tbsp. black bean sauce* (cha-chaung), 1 tbsp. honey, ½ tbsp brown suger, ½ tbsp. corn syrup

＊Note : Deep fried transparent noodles make a nice bedding for the hot chicken and a tasty addition in the lettuce wraps. Edible chrysanthemum leaves (sue-kaht) are also savory wrapped in lettuce.

1

2

3

Oyster and Pork Wrap

육 · 류 · 고 · 기 · 요 · 리 (Beef and meat dishes)

굴을 곁들인 돼지보쌈(Oyster and Pork Wrap)

준비는 이렇게(8~10인분)

돼지고기 2 lbs.(Top Loin Roast Bonless), 된장 3큰술, 마늘 5쪽, 생강 8쪽, 후추 1작은술, 마른 통고추 5개, 소금마늘가루 1작은술, 배추 ½포기, 소금 ¼작은술, 배추 잎사귀 1장, 물 10컵

만드는 것은 이렇게

❶ 냄비에 물 6컵을 붓고 배추를 제외한 모든 재료와 돼지고기를 넣고 2시간 정도 중간불에서 푹 삶는다.
❷ 건져내어 식은후에 편육으로 먹기좋은 크기로 썰어놓는다. (가로 1½인치, 세로 2½인치)
❸ 배추 ½포기는 냄비에 물 4컵을 붓고 소금 ¼작은술 넣고 간을 하여 끓이다가 손질한 배추를 넣고 30초 정도 데친 다음 찬물에 씻어 물기를 꼭 짠다.

굴무침 준비는 이렇게

굴 16 oz(454g), 무 1.08 lbs.(중간보다 약간 작은 크기), 볶은깨 1큰술, 고추가루 3½큰술, 소금마늘가루 1½큰술, 후추 ½작은술

굴무침은 이렇게

❶ 굴은 먼저 찬물에 잘 씻어 채에 받쳐둔다.
❷ 위에 소금마늘가루를 ½작은술 뿌려두고 무는 채썰어 고춧가루 2큰술로 빨갛게 물들인다.
❸ 물이 빠진 굴과 고춧가루 물든 무를 한데 넣고 다시 소금마늘가루(1큰술), 고춧가루(1½큰술), 후추(½작은술), 볶은깨(1큰술)를 넣고 잘 버무린다.

상차림은 이렇게

큰 접시에 배추를 먼저 깔고 그 다음에 돼지고기 편육을 질서있게 줄맞추어 놓고 데치지 않은 배추 잎사귀 1장 위에 버무려 놓은 굴무침을 놓고 상에 낸다. 먹을 때는 배추 위에 돼지고기, 그위에 굴무침을 먹기좋은 크기로 보쌈해서 먹으면 일품이다.

8~10 servings

1 lb. fresh oysters, ½ tsp. garlic salt, 1 lb. radish, cut into fine strips,1 tbsp. toasted sesame seeds*, 3½ tbsp. hot chili powder*,1 tbsp. garlic salt, ½ tsp. black pepper, 2 lbs. pork loin, boneless, 3 tbsp. Korean bean paste*, 5 cloves garlic, 8 slices ginger,1 tsp. black pepper, 5 dried hot chilies*, 1½ tbsp. garlic salt, ½ tsp. salt, ½ Chinese cabbage, 1 whole largeleaf, the rest cut lengthwise, 10cups water

Making

Rinse the oysters in cold water and sprinkle with ½ teaspoon garlic salt. Mix the radish strips with 2 tablespoons chili powder until they turn red. Toss the oysters and radishes with the toasted sesame seeds, remaining chili powder, 1 tablespoon garlic salt and pepper.
In a saucepan, cook the pork with 6 cups of water and the remaining ingredients, except the Chinese cabbage, for about 2 hours on medium heat. Remove the meat, saving the broth for later use. When the meat is cool, cut it in bite sized, wafer thin slices.
Put aside 1 large Chinese cabbage leaf, and blanch the remaining cabbage in 4 cups of water with ½ teaspoon salt. Rinse immediately with cold water to cool completely, then squeeze out any water. Cut the cabbage in wrapping sized (about 2″ x 3″) pieces.
On a serving platter, arrange the cabbage wrappers so they cover the platter. Place the cabbage leaf that is set aside in the center of the platter and mound the oysters on it. Arrange the pork slices on the wrappers around the oysters. Each diner may then place one or two oysters on a pork slice, wrap with the cabbage and enjoy.

＊ Available in Asian groceries.

돼지불고기(Spicy Barbeque Pork)

준비는 이렇게(4인분)

뼈없는 돼지고기 (살코기)1½ lb.

양념 준비는 이렇게

다진생강 1큰술, 다진마늘 2큰술, 참기름 2큰술, 고춧가루 ½큰술, 진 간장 ½큰술, 볶은고추장 2큰술, 정종 1큰술, 설탕 1큰술

만드는 것은 이렇게

❶ 돼지고기를 먹기좋은 크기(가로 1인치, 세로 3½인치, 두께 0.1인치)로 썬다.

❷ 양념 재료를 한데 섞어 양념장을 만들어 썰어놓은 돼지고기와 같이 무친다.

❸ 프라이팬에 판판히 놓고 굽기도 하고 오븐브로일로 굽든지 석 쇠에 구어도 된다.

* 프라이팬에 볶다가 야채(양파, 버섯(어떤 종류도 됨) , 당근 등)를 넣고 같이 볶으면 훌륭한 요리가 된다.

* 고기와 야채를 볶을 때는 반드시 고기를 먼저 익히고 야채를 넣어 볶는다.

4 servings

1½ lb. lean pork, 1 tbsp. minced ginger, 2 tbsp. minced garlic, 2 tbsp. sesame oil, ½ tbsp. hot chili powder*, ½ tbsp. dark soy sauce, 2 tbsp. seasoned hot chili paste*, 1 tbsp. rice wine (sake), 1 tbsp. sugar

Making

Slice the pork into thin bite-sized pieces. Combine the remaining ingredients and very gently mix into the pork. Barbeque the pork on a hot grill, broil under a broiler or cook (sizzle) in a hot preheated, ungreased skillet until done.

*Note : To the already cooked pork, add some vegetables such as onions, various kinds of mushrooms, carrots, etc., to create another tasty dish.

* Available in Asian groceries.

해 · 물 · 요 · 리 (Seafood dishes)

해물순두부 (Seafood with Soft Bean Curd)

준비는 이렇게(2인분)

두부 1모, 새우(중간크기)10개, 주꾸미 3마리(4OZ), 게살 2조각, 홍합 3개, 다진마늘 1큰술, 파 3뿌리, 고춧가루 1작은술, 양파(중간크기) ½, 불린 표고버섯이나 양송이 5개, 참기름 1큰술, 소금마늘가루 1작은술, 물 2컵

만드는 것은 이렇게

❶ 두부만 빼고 모든 재료들을 전부 잘게 썰거나 다져서 참기름 1 큰술에 2분 정도 볶는다.

❷ 물 2컵을 넣고 4,5분 끓이다가 물기를 뺀 두부를 뭉개서 부스러뜨려 넣은 다음 한번 더 끓인 후 소금마늘가루(갈릭솔트) 1작은술을 넣는다.

＊ 식성에 따라 소금마늘가루를 더 넣어도 되고 고춧가루를 더 넣든가 매운 것이 싫으면 아예 넣지 않아도 됨.

＊ 물대신 멸치국물이나 육수, 닭고기국물을 사용해도 됨.

2 servings

10 medium shrimp, shelled, deveined, coarsely chopped, 5 pieces baby octopus＊, chopped, 2 imitation crabsticks, chopped, 3-5 mussels, chopped, 1 tbsp. minced garlic, 3 spring onions, chopped, 1 tsp. hot chili powder＊, 1 small onion, chopped, 5 button mushrooms, chopped,1 tbsp. sesame oil, 2 cups water, 1 lb. soft bean curd＊,1 tsp. garlic salt

Making

Heat the sesame oil in a skillet and add the remaining ingredients except the water, bean curd and garlic salt. Stir-fry for 2 minutes. Add the water and boil for 4-5 minutes. Add the bean curd, crumbling it with fingers. When boiling, season with garlic salt.

＊Notes : The chili powder and garlic salt can be adjusted to individual taste. Meat, chicken or dried anchovy stock can be substituted for the water.

＊Available in Asian groceries.

해 · 물 · 요 · 리 (Seafood dishes)

매운새우와 매운조갯살 (Spicy Shrimp and Scallops)

🍳 준비는 이렇게(12인분)

중간크기의 새우와 Scallop(조갯살)을 합하여 1½ lbs., 녹말가루 2컵, 물 1컵, 달걀흰자 2개, 식용유 3컵

🍳 만드는 것은 이렇게

❶ 새우는 깨끗이 씻어 물기를 빼고, Scallop(조갯살)은 중간크기가 사방 1.3인치 정도 되므로 1개를 반으로 잘라 2쪽으로 새우와 비슷하게 한다.

❷ 녹말가루 ½컵에 새우와 Scallop(조갯살)을 묻혀두고 달걀흰자 2개를 잘 풀어 녹말가루 1½컵, 물 1컵에 반죽하여 녹말가루에 묻혀놓은 새우와 Scallop(조갯살)을 합하여 반죽해둔다.

❸ 식용유 3컵을 오목한 냄비에 붓고 끓어오를 때 새우와 Scallop(조갯살)을 튀겨낸 다음 한번 더 튀겨낸다.

❹ 판판한 프라이팬에 준비해 만들어 놓은 소스를 다 붓고 튀겨놓은 새우와 Scallop(조갯살)을 다 넣고 소스를 조심성있게 뒤적이면서 골고루 소스를 묻혀가며 볶는다.(2분정도)

🍳 소스 준비는 이렇게

닭국물이나 조갯국물 1½컵, 납작 썬 생강 8쪽, 다진 마늘 1½큰술, 물엿 2큰술, 참기름 3큰술, 설탕 3큰술, 포도주 1큰술, 정종 1작은술, Sweet Sour Sauce 2큰술, 고춧가루 1큰술, 진간장 2큰술, Sesame Chili Hot Sauce 2큰술, Sweet Chili Sauce 2큰술, 녹말가루 2큰술, 물 4큰술

🍳 소스 만드는 것은 이렇게

재료들을 전부 합하여 12분동안 팔팔 끓인 다음, 생강 8쪽은 버리고 물에 탄 녹말(녹말가루 2큰술, 물 4큰술)4큰술을 넣고 걸쭉하게 만든다.

＊ Sweet Chilli Sauce와 Sesame Chili Hot Sauce는 타일랜드 제품이며 동양식품에서 구입할 수 있음.

＊ 더욱 매운 것을 원할 때는 소스 끓일 때 마른 빨강통고추를 3개쯤 넣고 끓임

＊ Sweet & Sour Sauce는 중국제품(LACHOY 東)임.

🍳 12 servings

1½ lbs.shrimp and large sea scallops, 2 cups cornstarch, 1 cup water, 2 egg whites, 3 cups cooking oil for frying

🍳 Making

Clean and cut each shrimp lengthwise and each scallop horizontally in half. Pat dry and coat each piece with ½ cup of cornstarch.

In a mixing bowl, combine the egg whites, 1½ cups of cornstarch and 1 cup of water to make a batter. Heat the oil in a deep saucepan. Add the scallop and shrimp pieces to the batter. Quickly fry the pieces. For the best flavor and crispness, fry each piece twice.

In a saucepan, combine the seasoned sauce ingredients, except the cornstarch and water, and cook for 12 minutes. Discard the ginger and thicken the sauce with cornstarch mixed with water.

To serve, heat a skillet, add the seasoned sauce, fried shrimp and scallops, gently combine and heat through for 2 minutes.

🍳 For seasoned sauce

8 slices ginger, 1½ cups chicken broth or clam juice, 1 tbsp. minced garlic, 2 tbsp. prepared sweet sour sauce* (La Choy), 2 tbsp. corn syrup, 2 tbsp. prepared sweet chili sauce* (from Thailand), 3 tbsp. sesame oil, 2 tbsp. sesame chili hot sauce* (from Thailand), 3 tbsp. sugar, 1 tbsp. hot chili powder*, 1 tbsp. wine, 1 tsp. rice wine, 2 tbsp. soy sauce, 4 tbsp. water for cornstarch, 2 tbsp. cornstarch, 3 hot red chilies, dried* or fresh for added spiciness (optional)

＊ Sweet & Sour Sauce is available in Asian groceries (LACHOY 東)

1 2 3 4

해 · 물 · 요 · 리 (Seafood dishes)

연어 토막구이 (Pan-Fried Salmon)

준비는 이렇게(2인분)

연어 0.48 lb., 통마늘 3개(10피스), 생강 썬 것 15피스, 후추, 소금 섞은 것 ¼작은술, 식용유 3큰술

만드는 것은 이렇게

❶ 연어 토막을 잘 씻어 종이타월로 꼭꼭 눌러 물기를 뺀 다음 마늘과 생강(납작납작하게 썬것)10피스씩 준비해둔다.

❷ 생선위에 후추와 소금을 뿌리고 마늘, 생강10피스씩 생선 위(한쪽면)에 골고루 붙인다. 프라이팬에 식용유 3큰술을 두르고 생강 5쪽을 넣어 볶다가 연어토막을 마늘과 생강이 붙은 쪽으로 먼저 굽는다.

❸ 다 구운 뒤 마늘과 생강은 버린다.

＊ 식성에 따라 상에 낼 때 호두깐 것(작게 썰음)을 먹기전에 뿌려도 됨.

＊ 레몬 ¼쪽을 식성에 따라 쓸 수 있도록 같이 낸다.

2 servings

½ lb. salmon fillet, rinsed, patted dry, 3 cloves garlic, sliced in 10 pieces, 15 slices ginger, ¼ tsp salt, ¼ tsp pepper, 3 tbsp. cooking oil, lemon wedges and/or walnuts for garnish (optional)

Making

Sprinkle salt and pepper on the inside of the fillet, press in 10 slices of garlic and 10 of ginger. Heat oil in a skillet and stir-fry 5 slices of ginger. With the seasoned side down, pan-fry the salmon until the edges are cooked (turn opaque and slightly brown). Turn the fillet over and fry until done.

Remove the salmon from the skillet and discard the garlic and ginger. Serve with lemon wedges or sprinkle fried salmon with finely chopped walnuts, as preferred.

해 · 물 · 요 · 리 (Seafood dishes)

크게 썬 무, 갈치조림(Braised Ribbonfish with Radish)

준비는 이렇게(5인분)

은갈치 24 oz(680g), 무 1½ kg, 물 2½컵

만드는 것은 이렇게

❶ 갈치는 지느러미를 가위로 잘라 내고 칼집을 넣어 먹기좋은 크기로 잘라 놓는다.(12피스 정도로)
❷ 무는 깍둑썰기의 배로 크게 썬다. 넓은 냄비에 물 2½컵을 넣고 썰어놓은 무를 넣고 골고루 섞은 양념장을 ⅓정도 넣어 한소끔 끓이다가 갈치를 무 위에 쫙 놓고 남은 양념장을 골고루 뿌린 후 20분 정도 끓인다.

양념장은 이렇게

고추장 1큰술, 고춧가루 1큰술, 진간장 2큰술, 한국된장 ½큰술, 다진 마늘 1큰술, 흑설탕 ½큰술, 후추 1작은술

5 servings

1½ lbs. ribbonfish* (kahl-chi, a long, thin and silvery fish), 3 lbs. radish, (about 1½ kg.) cut 1″ x 2″ x ½″ thick, 2½ cups water, 1 tbsp. hot chili paste*, 1 tbsp. hot chili powder*, 1 tbsp. garlic, minced, ½ tbsp. brown sugar, 1 tsp. black pepper, 2 tbsp. soy sauce, ½ tbsp. Korean bean paste*

Making

If using frozen fish, it will already be cut into pieces. If using fresh fish, clean, discarding the head, tail and innards, and cut in 10-12 well rinsed pieces. Make a seasoning mixture by combining the remaining ingredients, except the radish and water.
Line the bottom of a saucepan with the radish, ⅓ of the seasoning mixture and the water. Bring to a boil, add the fish, spread the remaining seasoning over the pieces and cook on medium high heat for 20 minutes.

＊ Available in Asian groceries.

해 · 물 · 요 · 리 (Seafood dishes)

꼬타리 조림(Braised Pollack)

준비는 이렇게(8~10인분)

꼬타리 6마리(30-35토막), 물 8컵(64oz)

만드는 것은 이렇게

❶ 꼬타리는 지느러미와 꼬리를 가위나 칼로 깨끗하게 자른 뒤 토막을 낸다.

❷ 1마리가 5~6등분되게 자른 뒤 깨끗이씻어 납작한 냄비에 8컵의 물을 붓고 물이 끓을 때 꼬타리를 넣고 2분 정도 되면 채반에 쏟아 찬물에 헹군 다음 물기를 빼놓고, 판판한 프라이팬에 준비된 소스 재료만 먼저 넣고 3분 정도 볶다가 자작자작할 때 삶아 물기뺀 꼬타리를 넣는다.

❸ 양념이 골고루 잘 묻도록 넓은 주걱으로 조심성있게 들썩거리면서 2분 정도 볶은 뒤 접시에 담는다.

소스 준비는 이렇게

진간장 3큰술, 고춧가루 1큰술, 볶은깨 2큰술, 정종 2큰술, 참기름 3큰술, 물엿 2큰술, 흑설탕 2큰술, 포도주 1큰술, 오징어소스 2큰술, 감식초 1작은술, 후추 1작은술, 다진마늘 3큰술, 다진 생강 1큰술, 볶은고추장 1큰술(골고루 분량대로 잘 섞음)

＊꼬타리 생선을 물에 삶을 때 너무 오래 삶으면 생선이 부서지고 탄력성이 없어진다.

＊볶을 때 너무 휘저으면 고기가 부서지고 볼품이 없어진다.

＊오징어 소스는 타일랜드 제품이며 동양식품에서 구입.

8~10 servings

6 partially dried pollack*, 8 cups water

Making

Remove any fins and tails from the fish with kitchen shears. Rinse thoroughly and cut each pollack into 5 pieces, yielding 30 pieces in all. In a saucepan, bring water to a boil, add the pollack pieces and cook for 2 minutes. Drain in a colander, rinse in cold water and pat dry.
Make the seasoned soy sauce by combining the listed ingredients. In a skillet, heat the seasoned soy sauce until it splatters, about 3 minutes, and add the fish pieces, gently stirring to thoroughly coat and cook for 2 minutes.

For seasoned soy sauce

3 tbsp. soy sauce, 1 tbsp. hot chili powder*, 2 tbsp. rice wine, 2 tbsp. toasted sesame seeds, 3 tbsp. sesame oil, 2 tbsp. corn syrup, 2 tbsp. brown sugar, 1 tbsp. wine, 1 tsp. black pepper, 1 tsp. seasoned vinegar*, 3 tbsp. minced garlic, 1 tbsp. grated ginger, 2 tbsp. liquid from brined squid*, 1 tbsp. hot chili paste*

＊ Note : Overcooking the fish in boiling water or too much stirring in the seasoned soy sauce will cause the pieces to fall apart.

＊ Available in Asian groceries.

해 · 물 · 요 · 리 (Seafood dishes)

홍어무침(Spicy Raw Ray)

🥘 준비는 이렇게(6인분)

홍어 1 lb., 무 중간크기 1개, 당근 1개, 고추장 3큰술, 고춧가루 ½큰
술, 설탕 2큰술, 참기름 2 큰술, 식초(감식초) ½ 컵, 갖은양념(파3뿌리 –
잘게다짐, 다진마늘 2큰술, 다진생강 ½작은술, 깨소금 2큰술, 소금 ½
작은술)

🥘 만드는 것은 이렇게

❶ 홍어는 약간 언 상태에서 얇게 썰어 둔다.
❷ 썬 홍어를 식초에 담가 1시간 정도 둔다.
❸ 무와 당근은 채썰어 둔다.(무는 고춧가루에 물들임)
❹ 참기름과 식초만 빼고 고추장, 고춧가루, 설탕, 갖은 양념을 버
무려 놓는다. 식초에 담근 홍어를 두 번만 씻어 꼭 짠 뒤 갖은
양념을 넣고 맨 끝에 참기름을 넣는다.
❺ 신선한 맛, 향긋한 냄새를 위해 미나리나 오이를 먹기 전에 넣
으면 한결 좋다.
✱ 비빔냉면 국수에 곁들이면 훌륭한 회냉면이 됨.

🥘 6 servings

1 lb. ray✱, ½ cup vinegar, 1 medium radish, cut into thin strips, 1
carrot, cut into thin strips, 1 tbsp. hot red chili powder✱, 2 tbsp. sesame
oil, 3 tbsp. hot chili paste✱ oriental celery or cucumber, both cut into
thin strips (optional)

🥘 Making

To make slicing easy, place the ray in the freezer until icy but not
frozen. Slice the ray, thinly pour vinegar over the slices and let stand
for an hour. Rinse in cold water twice, then drain and gently squeeze
out any excess liquid.
Mix half the hot chili powder with the radish to dye it red. Then
thoroughly mix the carrot, chili paste, remaining chili powder and the
radish with the ray. Add the sesame oil as the finishing touch.

✱ Notes : Oriental celery (mi-nah-ri) and cucumbers will be refreshing
and aromatic if added just before serving.
When combined with buckwheat noodles, this recipe makes
another delicious noodle dish. (Hwae-nang-myun)
✱ Available in Asian groceries.

해 · 물 · 요 · 리 (Seafood dishes)

맛게살전(Crab Cakes)

준비는 이렇게(6인분)

게살 ½ lb., 파 1단(6뿌리), 달걀 2개, 소금 ½작은술, 참기름 ¼작은술, 밀가루 5큰술, 식용유, 물 5큰술

만드는 것은 이렇게

❶ 게살을 4등분하여 찢어놓고 파는 잘게 썬다.
❷ 달걀 2개에 밀가루 5큰술을 넣고 물 5큰술로 반죽한다.
❸ 반죽에 게살과 파를 넣고 참기름 ¼작은술을 넣은 다음 잘 저어둔다. 프라이팬에 식용유 2큰술을 두르고 게살반죽을 1스푼씩 놓은 다음 앞뒤가 노릇하게 지져낸다.

6 servings

2 eggs, 5 tbsp. flour, ½ tsp. salt, 5 tbsp. water, ½ lb. crab flavored sticks, quartered and shredded, 6 spring onions, chopped, ¼ tsp. sesame oil, 2 tbsp. cooking oil for frying

Making

In a mixing bowl, make a batter by combining the eggs, flour, salt and water. Add the shredded crab, spring onions and sesame oil, mixing well. Heat the cooking oil in a skillet, drop in spoonfuls of the crab mixture and fry both sides until nicely browned.

게살꼬치(Skewered Crabmeat)

준비는 이렇게(6인분)

게살 ½ lb., 파 6뿌리, 달걀 2개, 소금 ¼작은술, 꼬치 16개(6.5 cm길이), 밀가루 3큰술, 식용유

만드는 것은 이렇게

❶ 게살(김밥용 게살이 좋음)을 반으로 잘라 3등분(게살1개로 6등분되게)한다. 파는 게살길이와 같게 썰어놓는다.
❷ 꼬치에 게살, 파 순으로 끼우며 양쪽 끝에 게살이 가도록 꽂는다.
❸ 달걀 2개는 소금 간하여 잘 저어놓고 준비된 꼬치에 밀가루를 입힌 후 달걀에 골고루 묻혀 프라이팬에 식용유 2큰술을 두른 뒤 살짝 구워낸다.
＊ 게살전이나 게살꼬치는 중간불에서 굽는다.
  센불은 속이 익기 전에 바깥이 타고 곱지 않다.

6 servings

½ lb. imitation crabsticks, cut in thirds, then cut lengthwise to make 6 pieces, 6 spring onions, cut the same length as the crab, 2 eggs, ¼ tsp. salt, 3 tbsp. flour, 3 tbsp. cooking oil, 2½″ long bamboo skewers or strong toothpicks, as needed

Making

Beat eggs with a fork and salt lightly. On each skewer, alternate pieces of crabmeat and spring onion, ending with crabmeat. Dust the skewered items with flour, dip each skewer in the egg mixture and pan-fry both sides in a heated, well oiled skillet on medium heat. (High heat will burn the food before it is thoroughly cooked.)

황백 생선전

해 · 물 · 요 · 리 (Seafood dishes)

황백 생선전(Pan-Fried Yellow and White Fish Slices)

준비는 이렇게(6인분)

흰살 생선 1lb.(Orange Roughy), 계란 노른자 2개, 물 2큰술, 흰자 2개, 밀가루 ½컵, 소금 ½작은술, 파슬리 20잎, 붉은 통고추 20잎

만드는 것은 이렇게

❶ 생선은 적당한 크기로 자른 후 소금으로 밑간을 한다.(가로 3 인치, 세로 2.5인치)

❷ 달걀은 황,백으로 나눠 잘 저어둔다.(*흰자 위에는 밀가루를 약 간 넣어 저어둔다)

❸ 파슬리는 한잎씩 떼어 두고 붉은 고추는 둥근 모양대로 썰어둔 다.

❹ 밑간이 된 생선에 밀가루를 입혀 반으로 나누어둔다.

❺ 밀가루를 입힌 생선 반은 노른자물(노른자 2개에 물 2큰술 넣 어 묽게 만듦)을 묻혀 굽는다.

❻ 구울 때 파슬리잎을 위에 얹어 노릇하게 굽는다.

❼ 나머지 반은 흰자를 입혀 구우며 구울 때 붉은 고추를 동글동 글하게 썰어서 얹어 굽는다.

6 servings

1 lb. fish fillet (orange roughy), cut in 2½″ x 3″ x ¼″ slices, ½ tsp. salt, ½ cup flour, 2 egg yolks, lightly beaten, 2 tbsp. water for yolks, 2 egg whites, lightly beaten,1 tsp. flour for egg whites, 20 small parsley leaves, about ⅓ the size of a fish slice, 20 thin slices of red chili, seeded, ⅓ cup cooking oil for frying

Making

Season the fish slices with salt and coat with flour. In separate bowls, mix egg yolks with 2 tablespoons water and the egg whites with 1 teaspoon flour.

With half the fish slices, dip each slice in the egg yolk mixture, place in a heated, greased skillet and immediately add a parsley leaf and some chili slices on top and pan fry until done. Turn each stack over and fry the other side just a few seconds, not too long to change the color of the parsley or red chili slices.

Using the egg white mixture, repeat the process with other half of the fish slices.

아구찜(Braised Monk Fish, Agu Chim)

준비는 이렇게 (6인분)

아구 1마리(350~400g), 콩나물 454g, 파 5뿌리, 불린 고사리 100g, 미더덕 ½컵, 닭국물 ½컵, 피망 (빨강 ½ · 초록 ½), 녹말가루물 ½컵, 식용유 3큰술

만드는 것은 이렇게

❶ 아구생선은 내장을 빼고 잘 씻어 가위로 반을 자른 후 먹기좋은 적당 크기로 토막을 낸다.

❷ 콩나물은 머리와 꽁지를 따고 깨끗이 씻어 찜통에 4분 정도 쪄낸다.

❸ 파는 4센치 길이로 썬다. 피망(빨강, 초록)도 분량대로 썰어둔다.

❹ 미더덕은 소금물에 잘 씻어 몇 번 헹군 뒤 건져두고 고사리는 먹기좋은 크기로 가위로 잘라둔다.

❺ 양념재료들을 모두 잘 저어 골고루 섞는다.

❻ 납작하고 오목한 프라이팬에 식용유를 두르고 양념과 아구 토막을 넣고 볶는다.

❼ 아구가 어느 정도 익으면 닭국물(물을 써도 됨)을 부어 끓인 다음, 아구가 익으면 따로 건져둔다.(너무 계속 익으면 살이 부스러진다)

❽ 아구만 건져내고 남은 소스에 그대로 미더덕을 넣고 어느 정도 익으면 야채(콩나물, 피망(빨강 · 초록), 파, 고사리)를 넣고 볶다가 아구를 다시 넣어 볶는다.

❾ 끓고 있는 아구찜에 녹말가루물 ½컵을 조금씩 넣어가면서 걸쭉해질 때까지만 넣고 참기름 1큰술 넣고 맛을 낸후 상에 낸다.

양념 준비는 이렇게

고춧가루 3큰술, 진간장 1큰술, 닭국물 3큰술, 설탕 1작은술, 다진마늘 2큰술, 다진양파 3큰술, 다진생강 ½작은술, 볶은깨 1큰술, 후추 ⅓작은술, 참기름 1큰술, 정종 1½큰술

＊맛을 보고 싱거우면 맛소금을 쓴다.

6 servings

400g monkfish fillet, cut in large chunks, 3 tbsp. cooking oil, ½ cup chicken broth or water, ½ cup pre-soaked codoropsis*, washed in salted water, rinsed thoroughly and drained, 1 lb. soy bean sprouts, seed and root ends trimmed off, then blanched , 1½ spring onions, cut in ½″ long pieces, 1½ green pepper, cut in ½″ long pieces, 1½ red pepper cut in ½″ long pieces, 100g presoaked fern shoots*, cut in bite sized lengths, 2 tbsp. cornstarch, 4 tbsp. water to mix with cornstarch, 1 tbsp. sesame oil

Making

Combine the seasoning ingredients. In a heavy skillet, heat the cooking oil, add the seasoning and fish, and stir-fry until fish is seared. Add the chicken broth or water, bring to a boil, and when the fish is almost done, remove it to a plate.

Add the codoropsis to the skillet and cook until somewhat tender. Then add the remaining vegetables. Return the fish to the skillet, bring to a boil, and thicken with cornstarch mixed with water. As the final touch, add the sesame oil and serve.

For seasoning

3 tbsp. hot chili powder*, 1 tbsp. soy sauce, 3 tbsp. chicken broth, 1 tsp. sugar, 2 tbsp. minced garlic, 3 tbsp. onion, finely chopped, ½ tsp. grated ginger, 1 tbsp. toasted sesame seeds, ¼ tsp. black pepper, 1 tbsp. sesame oil, 1½ tbsp. rice wine

＊ Available in Asian groceries.

생선탕수육(Sweet and Sour Fish)

🐟 준비는 이렇게(4인분)

대구흰살생선 1lb., 녹말가루 1컵, 후추 ½작은술, 베이킹소다 ½작은술, 정종 ½큰술, 설탕 1큰술, 파인애플국물 ⅓컵, 소금 ½작은술, 생강 8쪽, 물 2½컵, 다진생강 ½작은술, Sweet & Sour Sauce 3큰술, 식초 ½작은술, 달걀흰자 1개, 식용유 3컵

🐟 만드는 것은 이렇게

❶ 생선살은 물기를 닦고 먹기좋은 크기(가로1.5인치, 세로1.5인치)로 썰어 녹말가루 ½컵에 후추 ½작은술, 생강 다진 것½작은 술, 베이킹소다 ½작은술 넣고 잘 버무려둔다.

❷ 녹말가루 ½컵에 달걀 흰자 1개를 잘 풀고 물 1컵을 넣어 튀김옷을 만들어 버무려둔 생선살을 넣어 혼합한 다음 끓는 식용유에 2번 튀겨낸다.

🐟 소스 만드는 것은 이렇게

❶ 납작납작하게 썬 8쪽의 생강과 물 1½컵을 붓고 10분 정도 매운냄새가 나도록 끓이면 생강물 1컵이 된다.

❷ 생강은 버리고 생강물에 정종½큰술, Sweet & Sour Sauce 3큰술, 설탕 1큰술, 소금 ½작은술, 식초 ½작은술, 파인애플국물 ⅓컵을 넣고 끓인 다음 물에 탄 녹말가루(녹말가루1큰술, 물 ½컵)를 조금씩 조금씩 넣으면서 걸쭉하게 되면 불을 끈다.

✳ 접시에 튀겨놓은 생선을 담고 위에 골고루 소스를 뿌린다.

✳ 고명으로 빨간 피망 ½쪽, 노란 피망 ½쪽을 굵게 채썬다.

✳ 파란 완두콩 1큰술, 잣 1큰술을 다 준비된 생선 탕수육 위에 얹는다.

✳ 식성에 따라 고명을 다르게 해도 됨.

✳ Sweet & Sour Sauce는 중국제품(LACHOY 東)임.

🐟 4 servings

1 lb. fish (preferably white fish), cut bite-size, 1 cup cornstarch, ½ tsp. black pepper, ½ tsp. baking powder, ½ tsp. minced ginger, 1 egg white, 2½ cup water, 3-4 cups oil for frying
garnishes (optional): strips of red and yellow pepper, peas or pine nuts

🐟 Making

Season the fish with a mixture of ½ cup cornstarch, black pepper, baking powder and minced ginger. Make a batter by mixing ½ cup cornstarch, egg white and 1 cup water. Add fish and dredge thoroughly to coat. Heat oil and fry the fish, carefully dropping in one piece at a time so they do not stick together. Remove fish and keep warm in the oven. For crispness, fry the fish twice.
Prepare the sauce by boiling 1½ cups water and the ginger slices for 10 minutes or until reduced to 1 cup of liquid (called ginger water) and a strong ginger aroma has emerged. Discard the ginger. Add the remaining sauce ingredients, except the cornstarch and ½ cup water, and bring to a boil. Thicken with cornstarch mixed with water.
To serve, gently toss the fried fish with the sauce. Garnish with a few strips of red and yellow pepper, peas or pine nuts to taste.

🐟 For sauce

8 slices ginger, 1½ cups water, 1 tbsp. sugar, 3 tbsp. ready made sweet and sour sauce, ½ tbsp. sake (rice wine), ½ tsp. vinegar, ⅓ cup pineapple juice, 1 tbsp. cornstarch, ½ tsp salt

✳ Sweet & Sour Sauce is available in Asian groceries (LACHOY 東)

골뱅이 해초 무침(Conch and Fresh Kelp Salad)

🍲 준비는 이렇게(15인분)

골뱅이통조림(7.05oz, 200g), 무(중간크기) ½쪽, 식초 1큰술, 설탕 1½ 큰술, 소금 ½작은술, 채썬 당근 1컵, 불린 표고버섯 2장, 캬베츠(중간크기) ¼쪽, 게맛살(8센티) 13개, 해초무침(양념된 것) 1컵, 씨없는 긴 오이 1개, 명태채 6oz(170g), 미나리 0.25 lb., 가는 당면 1.3oz(37.5g), 물 3컵

🍲 만드는 것은 이렇게

❶ 무는 채썰어 식초1큰술, 설탕 1½큰술, 소금 ½작은술을 넣고 주물러 10분 정도 숨을 죽인 다음 꼭 짜서 물기를 뺀다.
❷ 당근과 불린 표고버섯은 채썰고 표고버섯만 소금 약간 넣어 살짝 볶아놓는다. 생강도 4쪽 썰어 놓는다.
❸ 캬베츠 ¼쪽을 줄기는 떼어내고 채썰어 놓는다.
❹ 게맛살(8센티)은 잘 찢어 놓는다. (13피스)
❺ 양념된 해초무침 1컵을 준비한다.
❻ 씨없는 긴 오이는 채썰어 놓는다.
❼ 통조림 골뱅이는 먹기좋은 크기로(1센티) 길쭉하게 썰어 놓는다.
❽ 명태채는 길이가 8센티 정도 되므로 3등분씩 썰어놓는다.
❾ 미나리를 깨끗이 씻어 3센티 길이로 썰어놓는다.
❿ 가는당면(찌개용) 1.3oz(37.5g)은 끓는 물에 삶아 먹기좋은 크기로 썰어 채반에서 물기를 뺀다.
⓫ 위의 모든 재료가 준비되면 판판한 그릇에 ❶~❿까지 모두 담고 잘 섞어둔 양념장을 골고루 넣고 버무려 상에 낸다.

🍲 양념장 준비는 이렇게

파 3뿌리(잘게 다짐), 다진마늘 2큰술, 생강 4쪽, 볶은깨 3큰술, 볶은 고추장 2큰술, 식초 2큰술, 설탕 3큰술, 후추 ½작은술, 참기름 3큰술, 풋고추 3개(잘게 다짐), 소금마늘가루 ½큰술

✳ 해초무침은 한국제품 또는 일본제품도 있어 동양식품점에서 구입 할 수 있다.
✳ 통조림 골뱅이도 동양식품점에 있다.

🍲 15 servings

7oz. steamed conch* from a 200g can, cut in bite size slices, ½ medium radish, cut in thin strips, 1 tbsp. vinegar, 1½ tbsp. sugar, ½ tsp. salt, 1 cup carrot strips, 2 black mushrooms softened in water, drained, cut in strips, ¼ medium cabbage, cored, the thick stems removed, and cut in strips, 13 crabstick pieces, each 3″ long, shredded, 1 cup seasoned kelp salad* (commercially prepared), 1 seedless cucumber, cut in strips, 6 oz. dried shredded pollack*, cut in 1″ long pieces, ¼ lb. Chinese celery*, cut in 3″ long pieces, 1.3oz. thin transparent noodles

🍲 Making

Marinate the radish in a mixture of vinegar, sugar and salt for 10 minutes and then gently squeeze out any liquid. Saute the mushrooms with a pinch of salt. Cook the noodles in boiling water, rinse, drain in a colander and, with kitchen shears, snip several times into random pieces. Combine all the ingredients listed for the dressing and set aside. When ready to serve, arrange the various prepared ingredients on a large platter. At the table, toss with the dressing and enjoy.

🍲 For the dressing

2 tbsp. minced garlic, 3 spring onions, finely chopped, 2 tbsp. vinegar, 3 tbsp. toasted sesame seeds, 3 tbsp. sugar, ½ tsp. black pepper, 3 tbsp. sesame oil, 3 green chilies, finely chopped, ½ tbsp. garlic salt, 2 tbsp. hot chili paste*, 4 pieces ginger

✳ Available in Asian groceries.

해파리냉채(Cold Jellyfish Salad)

🍤 준비는 이렇게 (6인분)

해파리 ½lb, 씨없는 오이 1개, 삶은새우(중간크기) 15마리, 잣 ½큰술

🍤 만드는 것은 이렇게

❶ 해파리는 먼저 소금을 털고 짠맛을 뺄 때, 물에 잠길 정도로 물을 부어 우려낸다.

❷ 2~3번 물을 갈아준다.

❸ 70° 정도의 뜨거운 물에 데쳐낸다. (팔팔 끓는 물에 데치면 오그라들고 쪼그라들어 볼품이 없다)

❹ 데친 해파리를 식초 1큰술, 설탕 1½큰술에 20분 정도 재어둔다.

❺ 다시 찬물에 헹군 다음 먹기 좋은 크기로 긴 것만 적당히 가위로 자른다.

❻ 깨끗이 씻은 오이를 4~5센티 길이로 채썬다.

❼ 새우는 위에서 아래로 반으로 저며 자른다.(1개를 길이로 2등분함)

❽ 채썬 오이와 새우, 해파리를 함께 섞어 차게 냉장고에 두었다가 먹기 직전에 혼합한 마늘양념을 넣고 버무린 다음 접시에 담아내고 잣을 뿌린다.

🍤 마늘 양념은 이렇게

다진마늘 2큰술, 식초 4큰술, 설탕 3½큰술, 진간장 1큰술, 소금 ½작은술, 참기름 1큰술

* 마늘은 칼등으로 쳐서 납작하게 으깬 뒤 입자가 보이게 굵게 다진다.

* 참기름을 너무 많이 쓰면 시원한 맛이 없다.

* 기호에 따라 싱거우면 소금으로 간한다.

🍤 6 servings

½lb jellyfish*, 1 tbsp. vinegar, 1½ tbsp. sugar, 15 cooked shrimp, each cut lengthwise in half, 1 cucumber, cut in thin strips, ½ tbsp. pine nuts for garnish

🍤 Making

Soak the jellyfish in enough water to cover and change the water 2-3 times to remove the brine. Blanch the jellyfish in hot (70C) but not boiling water (boiling water will cause jellyfish to shrink and toughen). Combine the jellyfish with the vinegar and sugar and let stand for 20 minutes. Rinse in cold water. Cut in bite sized pieces and keep cold in the refrigerator along with cucumbers and shrimp.

Mix the dressing ingredients. Just before serving, gently and thoroughly toss the seafood and cucumbers with the dressing. Adjust the salt and garnish with pine nuts.

🍤 For the dressing

2 tbsp. chopped garlic, 4 tbsp. vinegar, 3½ tbsp. sugar, 1 tbsp. soy sauce, ½ tsp. salt, 1 tbsp. sesame oil

✳ Note : Too much sesame oil will decrease the freshness of the flavors.

✳ Available in Asian groceries.

오징어젓(Pickled Squid)

🦪 준비는 이렇게

오징어 2마리(24oz.), 식초 1컵, 소금 1큰술

🦪 만드는 것은 이렇게

❶ 소스는 재료를 합하여 바글바글 2분정도 끓여 완전히 식혀둔다.

❷ 오징어는 다리를 떼어버리고 배를 갈라 내장을 제거한 뒤 껍질을 벗기고 깨끗이 씻어 채썰어 놓는다.(가로 0.2인치, 세로 2인치)

❸ 채썬 오징어를 국수채반에 담고 흐르는 찬물에 계속 주무르면서 채반 밑으로 물이 계속 빠지도록 물을 그대로 틀어놓고 문질러주면 거품이 빠지면서 오징어가 하얗게 깨끗하게 된다.

❹ 깨끗하고 물기없는 오징어에 1컵의 식초를 붓고 다시 주물러 거품을 빼고 찬물에 헹구면서 채반에 물이 빠지도록 한 다음 꼭 짠 뒤 소금 1큰술을 넣고 잘 혼합한 뒤 30분쯤 지나 소금에 절인 오징어를 두손으로 소금기와 물기를 꼭 짜고난 다음 비닐봉지에 봉하여 냉장고에 넣고 하룻밤을 재운 뒤에 만들어놓은 소스와 같이 섞어 잘 버무려 꼭꼭 눌러두면 다음날부터 먹을 수 있다.

❺ 냉장고에 보관해서 먹으면 더욱 신선하다.

🦪 소스 준비는 이렇게

고추장 3큰술, 다진마늘 2큰술, 다진생강 1작은술, 물엿 3큰술, 고춧가루 1큰술, 포도주 1작은술

🦪 serving

2squid, fresh or frozen and thawed, 1 cup vinegar, 1 tbsp. salt

🦪 Making

Slit each squid open, remove the central bone or beak, tentacles and innards. Pull off the skin and cut the remaining body into thin 2″ strips. Place strips in colander and rinse under running water, washing by hand until the water runs clean. Sprinkle with vinegar and mix them by hand until bubbles and foam appear. Then rinse the squid strips again in cold running water until clear. Drain and shake off any excess water. In a bowl, combine the squid with the salt, let stand for 30 minutes, then squeeze out the resulting liquid. Store over night in a plastic bag.

The next day, combine all the ingredients for the pickling seasoning and boil for 2 minutes. Let cool.

Mix with squid with the pickling seasoning and let stand at room temperature for a day. Thereafter, the dish is ready to eat and should be kept refrigerated.

🦪 For pickling seasoning

3 tbsp. hot chili paste*, 2 tbsp. minced garlic, 1 tsp. grated ginger, 3 tbsp. corn syrup, 1 tbsp. hot chili powder*, 1 tsp. wine

✻ Available in Asian groceries.

해 · 물 · 요 · 리 (Seafood dishes)

오징어 장어구이(Broiled Squid)

🍲 준비는 이렇게(4인분)

오징어(중간 크기) 2마리

🍲 만드는 것은 이렇게

❶ 깨끗이 장만한 오징어를 배쪽으로 판판하게 펴놓고 칼집을 역
  4각형으로 비스듬히 넣은 뒤 2쪽으로 잘라 만들어 놓은 소스
  (오징어강정소스와 같음)를 붓으로 바른 뒤 오븐에 10분 정도
  구워낸다. 만약 튀긴 오징어를 쓸 경우에도 소스는 똑같이
  발라 구워낸다.
❷ 3분 정도 간격에 소스를 앞 뒤로 골고루 3번 정도 발라준다.
❸ 먹기 좋은 크기로 썰어 레몬(큰술 1) + 간장(큰술 1½) 배합
  으로 찍어먹는다.

🍲 양념장 준비는 이렇게

레몬 1큰술, 간장 1큰술, 꿀 ½큰술

* 소스 만드는 법 : 오징어강정 소스 만드는 것과 같다.

🍲 4 servings

2 medium sized squid, peeled, cleaned, innards removed, 1 tbsp.
lemon juice, 1½ tbsp. soy sauce

🍲 Making

Slit the squid open and flatten the body with the inside facing
upward. Holding the knife at a 45-degree angle, score a trellis pattern
across the squid, and cut into 4 pieces. Mix the lemon juice and soy
sauce and set aside.

Make the sauce by boiling the water with ginger until reduced to a ½
cup. Discard the ginger and add all the remaining sauce ingredients.
Boil for 2-3 minutes.

Brush the squid with the sauce and broil under a broiler for 10 minutes,
turning the pieces several times and brushing with sauce every 3
minutes. Cut into bite size morsels and serve with the lemon juice and
soy sauce mixture on the side.

🍲 For sauce

2 cups water, 12 slices ginger, 1 tbsp. oyster sauce, 2 tbsp. corn
syrup, 2 tbsp. dark soy sauce, 2 tbsp. sesame oil, 10 slices garlic, 1 tsp.
wine, 1 tbsp. lemon juice, 1 tbsp. sugar, 1 tbsp. squid sauce*

* Note : Sauce is the same as for Oh-jing-a Kahng-jeung (fried squid).
* Available in Asian groceries.

오징어강정(Fried Squid Dish)

🍲 준비는 이렇게(5인분)

물오징어 2 마리, 녹말가루 ½ 컵, 후추 ½ 작은술, 식용유 3컵, 마른 빨강 통고추 3~5개

🍲 만드는 것은 이렇게

❶ 오징어를 껍질을 벗기고 다리는 떼어 내고 몸통만 깨끗이 장만 한 다음 물기를 뺀 후에 가로0.5인치, 세로1인치로 썰어 녹말 가루 ½컵에 후추 ½작은술과 오징어를 묻혀놓는다.

❷ 10분 정도 뒤에 튀김옷 재료들을 반죽한 것과 혼합하여 오목 한 냄비에 식용유 3컵을 붓고 끓어오를 때 반죽한 오징어를 튀 겨내고 한번 더 튀겨낸다.(2번 튀김)

🍲 튀김옷은 이렇게

물 1⅓컵, 밀가루 1컵, 녹말가루 ½ 컵, 달걀 흰자 1개, 베이킹소다 1작은술

🍲 소스 준비는 이렇게

생강 12쪽(세로 1인치,가로 0.5인치), 물 2컵, Oyster Sauce 1큰술, 물엿 2 큰술, 진간장 2큰술, 참기름 2큰술, 마늘 10쪽(마늘 2개), 포도주 1작은술, 설탕 2큰술, 오징어소스 1큰술, 레몬 1큰술

🍲 소스 만드는 것은 이렇게

❶ 물 2컵에 생강12쪽을 넣고 15분 정도 끓여 생강물이 줄어 ½ 컵이 되면 생강은 버리고 생강물에 나머지 재료들을 다 넣고 2~3분 정도 끓인다.

❷ 판판한 프라이팬에 만들어 놓은 소스를 붓고 1분쯤 되어 보글 보글 끓을 때 튀겨놓은 오징어를 다 넣고 프라이팬을 들고 몇 번 흔들거나 넓은 주걱으로 소스가 골고루 가도록 잘 젓는다.

❸ 불을 끄면서 마른 빨강 통고추를 3~5개 넣고 상에 낸다. 깨 를 뿌린다.

＊ 무리하게 젓가락 같은 것으로 휘저어 볶으면 튀김옷이 다 벗겨진다.

🍲 5 servings

2 fresh squid, without tentacles, peeled and cleaned, ½ cup cornstarch, ½ tsp. black pepper, 3 cups oil for frying, 3-5 dried red chilies, sesame seeds for garnish

🍲 Making

Dry any excess moisture from squid, cut into 1″ x ½″ pieces, and coat with ½ cup cornstarch and black pepper. Let stand for 10 minutes.

Combine the batter ingredients and mix well. Mix in the squid and fry pieces in small batches, placing them one by one in the hot oil to prevent their sticking together. For crispness, fry the squid twice.

Make the sauce by boiling the water with the ginger until reduced to a ½ cup. Discard the ginger and add all the remaining ingredients. Boil for 2-3 minutes.

In a large skillet, bring the sauce to a boil and add the fried squid, shaking the skillet a few times to coat well with the sauce. Remove from heat and add dried red chilies. Garnish with toasted sesame seeds.

🍲 For batter

½ cup cornstarch, 1 cup flour, 1⅓ cups water, 1 egg white, 1 tsp. baking soda.

🍲 For sauce

2 cups water, 12 slices ginger, 1 tbsp. oyster sauce, 2 tbsp. corn syrup, 2 tbsp. dark soy sauce, 2 tbsp. sesame oil, 10 slices garlic, 1 tsp. wine, 1 tbsp. lemon juice, 2 tbsp. sugar, 1 tbsp. squid sauce*

＊ Note : When combining the fried squid with sauce, be very gentle other wise batter may come off the squid.

＊ Available in Asian groceries.

해 · 물 · 요 · 리 (Seafood dishes)

오징어 야채무침(Squid Salad)

🍲 준비는 이렇게

오징어(중간 크기) 1마리, 당근 1개(꽃모양), 풋고추 3개(어슷썰기), 양파(중간 크기) 1½ - (큼직하게 반달형 썰기), 마늘 1쪽(잘게 다짐), 흰 깨 1큰술, 참기름 1½큰술, 까만깨 1작은술, 식초 1½작은술, 설탕 1½ 큰술, 볶음 고추장 1½큰술, 물 4컵

🍲 만드는 것은 이렇게

❶ 오징어는 껍질을 벗기고 내장을 제거한 뒤에 깨끗이 씻어 판판 한 냄비에 물4컵이 팔팔 끓을 때 넣어 데친 후 물에 데친 오징 어를 손가락 마디만큼(가로0.5인치,세로 2.5인치) 잘라 식힌 후 에 모든 재료를 넣고 골고루 무친다.

❷ 풋고추나 양파, 당근 등은 큼직큼직하게 썰어 넣는다.

🍲 serving

1 squid (medium size), peeled, cleaned, innards removed, 3 green chilies, cut in chunks, 1½ medium onions, cut in chunks, 1 carrot, cut in flower shapes, 4cups water

🍲 Making

Blanch the squid in boiling water. Remove and cut in thumb sized bites and let cool. Combine the seasoning ingredients thoroughly and gently mix in the squid. Add the green chilies, onions and carrot flowers and serve.

🍲 For seasoning

1 clove garlic, minced, 1 tbsp. sesame seeds, toasted, 1½ tbsp. sesame oil, 1 tsp. black sesame seeds, 1½ tsp vinegar, 1½ tbsp. hot chili paste, 1½ tbsp. sugar

생굴무침 (Oysters with Radish)

🦪 준비는 이렇게

생굴 1 lb.(16 oz, 454g), 무,중간크기½쪽(400g), 볶은깨 2큰술, 고춧가루 4큰술, 소금 1큰술, 후추 ½작은술, 볶은까만깨 ½큰술

🦪 만드는 것은 이렇게

❶ 냉동생굴을 2시간 정도 밖에 내놓으면 얼음이 녹는다.
❷ 깨끗이 씻어 소금 ½큰술, 후추 ½작은술을 뿌리고 물기를 뺀다.
❸ 무는 껍질을 벗기고 채썰어 고춧가루 2큰술에 물들인다.
❹ 물기를 빼놓은 굴과 채썰어 고춧가루에 물들여 놓은 무와 볶은 깨(흰깨)를 한 데 넣고 소금½큰술, 고춧가루2큰술을 넣은 뒤 잘 주물러 병에 담아 냉장고에 보관하면 다음날 먹을 수 있다. 3일 안에 다 먹어야 된다.

🦪 serving

1 lb. oysters, 1 tbsp. salt, ½ tsp. black pepper, ½ radish (400g), 4 tbsp. hot chili powder*, 2 tbsp. sesame seeds, toasted, ½ tbsp. toasted black sesame seeds (optional)

🦪 Making

Thaw frozen oysters at room temperature for 2 hours. Rinse, add ½ tablespoon salt and the black pepper, then drain excess water. Peel the radish, cut in thin strips and add 2 tablespoons chili powder to dye them red. Combine the oysters, radish, remaining chili powder, salt and the sesame seeds. Store in the refrigerator and serve the next day. (This dish will remain good for up to three days.)

∗ Available in Asian groceries.

해 · 물 · 요 · 리 (Seafood dishes)

팔보채(Eight Treasures Dish, Paul Boh Chai)

😋 준비는 이렇게(4인분)

쇠고기(½lb.) 편육 10쪽, 돼지고기(½lb.) 편육 10쪽, 오징어 ½마리, 삶은 새우 12개, 홍합 6쪽, 불린 표고버섯 12쪽, 어묵 8조각, 불린 해삼 4개, 작은옥수수통조림 4oz., 당근 1개, 양파 ½개, 파 2쪽

😋 만드는 것은 이렇게

❶ 쇠고기 ½lb.는 기름없는 것으로 물 2컵에 15분 정도 끓여 젓가락이 순하게 들어갈 때까지 삶고 국물은 기름을 걷어 육수로 쓰고 고기는 가로 1.5, 세로2.5인치 정도 크기로 썰어놓는다.

❷ 돼지고기도 쇠고기의 방법대로 삶아 같은 크기로 썰어놓는다.

❸ 돼지고기 삶은 국물은 버린다.

❹ 오징어는 껍질을 벗기고 배쪽으로 사방 칼집을 넣어 비늘같이 무늬를 넣어 삶으면 된다.

❺ 물 2컵이 끓을 때 오징어를 넣고 1~2분정도 후에 건져내어 찬물에 헹구어 가로 1인치,세로 2인치 정도로 썰어놓는다.

❻ 삶은 새우는 껍질이 있으면 벗기고 없으면 그냥 물기를 뺀다.

❼ 홍합은 잘 씻어 물기를 빼고 불린 표고버섯은 잘 씻어 꼭지를 떼고 굵직하게 채썰어 놓는다.

❽ 나무판에 붙어 있는 어묵은 ½을 납작납작하게 썰어놓는다.

❾ 물에 불린 해삼은 찌꺼기를 잘 떼어내고 내장도 잘 손질해서 큼직큼직하게(가로 1.5인치, 세로 2.5인치 정도)썰어놓는다.

❿ 작은옥수수통조림도 반씩 잘라놓는다.(8조각을 잘라 16조각되게)

⓫ 당근은 껍질을 벗기고 3등분하여 길이로 4쪽을 내면 12조각이 된다. 톱니모양으로 칼집을 넣어 모양낸다.

⓬ 양파는 껍질을 벗기고 잘 씻은 후에 반달형으로 썰고 파 2쪽도 어슷어슷 2인치 길이로 썰어놓는다.

😋 팔보채 볶기

❶ 판판하고 오목한 큰 프라이팬에 참기름 2큰술을 넣고 잘잘 소리날 때 납작납작하게 썬 마늘 12쪽을 넣고 볶다가 육수나 닭고기국물 1컵에 녹말가루 1큰술을 혼합하여 참기름과 마늘볶는 데 넣는다.

❷ 걸쭉하게 될 때까지 골고루 잘 젓는다.

❸ 육수와 녹말가루 섞은 것이 익을 때쯤 준비해 놓은 나머지 소스 재료를 다 넣고 그 다음에 야채만 뺀 준비한 재료들을 다 넣는다.

❹ 1분 정도 지나 계속 볶으면서 당근과 양파, 작은옥수수, 파를 넣고 참기름 1큰술 넣고 불을 끄고 접시에 담아낸다.

＊식성과 맛에 따라 굴소스를 좀더 써도 되고 조개다시다를 좀 써도 해물냄새의 향이 더 난다.

＊굴소스는 동서양 식품점에 있으므로 쉽게 구입할 수 있음.

＊불린 해삼은 중국식품점에 가면 구입할 수 있음.

😋 소스 준비는 이렇게

육수 또는 닭국물 1컵, 굴소스 1½큰술, 다진생강 ½큰술, 마늘 4개, (납작 썬 것 12쪽), 다진마늘 1큰술, 참기름 3큰술, 정종 ½큰술, 후추 ½ 작은술, 녹말가루 1큰술

😋 4 servings

½ lb. lean beef, ½ lb. lean pork, ½ squid tube*, 12 cooked shrimp, 6 mussels, cooked and shelled, 4 sea cucumbers*, softened in water like gelatin and cleaned, 8 slices colorful steamed fish cake* (comes on a wooden board), 12 black mushrooms, softened in water and cut in halves, 1 carrot, quartered lengthwise and cut into 12 sticks, ½ onion, sliced to form disks, 2 spring onions, cut into 2″ long pieces, 8 cobs baby corn from tin*, each cut lengthwise (16 pieces), water

😋 Making

Boil the beef in 2 cups of water for 2 minutes, and then simmer 12-13 minutes until tender. Remove beef and slice into 10 thin slices, each about1½″ x 2½″. Reserve stock for later use. Repeat the same method with the pork to make 10 thin slices. Slit the squid to open it and lay it flat with the inside facing up. Holding the knife at a 45-degree angle to the working surface and score the squid in a trellis pattern; blanch squid in boiling water for 1-2 minutes, rinse in cold water, then cut into 1″ x 2″ pieces. Cut the sea cucumber in similar sized pieces as squid.

Make the sauce in a large skillet by heating 2 tablespoons of sesame oil and stir-frying the garlic until light brown. Dissolve the cornstarch in the broth and add to the skillet with the remaining sauce ingredients. When the sauce thickens, add the beef, pork, squid, shrimp, mussels, sea cucumber, fish cake and black mushrooms. Cook until heated thoroughly and well coated with sauce. Add the remaining vegetables and cook for 1 minute. Stir in 1 tablespoon of sesame oil as a finishing touch.

😋 For sauce

3 tbsp. sesame oil, 4 cloves garlic, sliced into 12 pieces, 1 cup broth, meat or chicken, 1 tbsp. cornstarch, 1½ tbsp. oyster sauce*, ½ tbsp. minced ginger, 1 tbsp. minced garlic, ½ tsp. sake (rice wine), ½ tsp. black pepper

＊Notes : Oyster sauce can be adjusted to individual taste.
Shellfish Broth Mix* (Dah-shi-dah) can be added to enhance the seafood flavor.

＊Available in Asian groceries.

해삼탕(Sea Cucumber Dish, Hae-Sham Tang)

🍲 준비는 이렇게(4인분)

불린해삼 6마리, 삶은새우 20마리, 물오징어 ½마리, 불린표고버섯 (큰것)3개, 통조림버섯(strawmushrooms) 1.5oz, 당근(작은것)1개, 배추줄기 1개, 파 3뿌리, 통마늘10쪽, 생강 4쪽, 참기름 4큰술, 진간장 3큰술, 녹말가루 3큰술, 물 4큰술

🍲 만드는 것은 이렇게

❶ 불린 해삼은 잘 씻어(해삼 불리면 4인치~5인치 정도이므로) 2등분하여 (가로 1인치, 세로 2.5인치 정도) 썰어둔다.

❷ 삶은 새우는 껍질이 있으면 벗기고(없는 경우가 더 많다) 물기를 빼고 준비한다.

❸ 오징어 ½마리는 물 2컵, 팔팔 끓을 때 넣고 삶아 찬물에 씻어 가로 1인치, 세로 2인치로 썰어둔다.

❹ 3시간 이상 물에 불린 표고버섯은 꼭지를 따고 굵직하게 채썰어둔다.

❺ 통조림버섯은 물기를 빼고 준비한다.

❻ 당근은 껍질을 벗기고 3등분하여 길이로 잘라 톱니모양으로 모양을 낸다.

❼ 배추 1줄기는 잘 씻어 길쭉길쭉 당근 크기로 썰어놓고 파도 어슷어슷 배추길이로 썰어놓는다.

❽ 마늘은 납작납작하게 30쪽 정도 썰어놓는다.

❾ 생강도 납작하게 4쪽만 준비한다.

❿ 녹말가루 3큰술에 물 4큰술을 잘 혼합해둔다.

🍲 해삼탕 볶는법

❶ 판판한 프라이팬이나 큼직한 냄비에 마늘 30피스를 먼저 넣고 참기름 4큰술을 넣고 썰어놓은 생강 4쪽을 넣고 자작자작 소리날 때 불린 해삼을 넣고 1분 정도 볶는다.

❷ 볶다가 표고버섯, 통조림 버섯, 오징어, 새우 순서로 한 가지씩 넣어가며 볶다가 간장 3큰술을 넣고 물에 타놓은 녹말가루를 조금씩 조금씩 걸쭉할 때까지 볶다가 마지막에 야채(배추,당근,파)를 넣고 불을 끄고 상에 낸다.

＊진한 맛을 원하면 조개다시다를 써도 무방함.

＊불린 해삼은 중국식품점에 가면 구입할 수 있음.

＊버섯은 양송이 버섯을 써도 됨.

🍲 4 servings

6 sea cucumbers* (each 4-5″ long), soaked and softened, ½ fresh squid, peeled and cleaned, or squid tube*, 4 tbsp. sesame oil, 10 cloves garlic, sliced to make 30 pieces,
4 slices ginger, 3 black mushrooms, softened in water and cut into thick strips, 1.5 oz. straw mushrooms, from a tin*, drained, 20 cooked shrimp, 1 carrot, cut into long, wide strips, 1 leaf Napa cabbage, white stalk only, sliced like the carrot, 3 spring onions cut lengthwise as long as the carrot, 3 tbsp. soy sauce, 3 tbsp. cornstarch, 4 tbsp. water

🍲 Making

Rinse the sea cucumber thoroughly and cut into 1″x 2½″ pieces. Blanch the squid in 2 cups of boiling water, rinse in cold water and then cut into 1″ x 2″ pieces.
In a heavy skillet, heat the sesame oil and stir-fry garlic slices and ginger until they spatter in the pan. Add the sea cucumbers and cook for one minute. Stirring constantly, add the black mushrooms, straw mushrooms, squid and then the shrimp in this order.
Combine soy sauce, cornstarch and water, and add this mixture to the skillet to thicken. Next, gently stir in the carrot, cabbage and spring onion. Remove from heat and serve.

＊Note : Shellfish Broth Mix* will enhance the flavor of seafood.

＊Available in Asian groceries.

해물파전

해 · 물 · 요 · 리 (Seafood dishes)

해물파전 (Pan-Fried Spring Onion Patties with Seafood)

🍲 준비는 이렇게(4인분)

파 100g, 쇠고기 간 것 35g, 잔새우 50g, 게맛살 2쪽, 조갯살 30g, 오징어 50g, 피망 ½쪽, 밀가루 1컵, 닭국물 1컵, 소금 ½작은술, 후추 ½작은술, 볶은깨 1작은술, 참기름 1큰술, 달걀 1개, 식용유 ⅓컵 (2.7oz.)

🍲 만드는 것은 이렇게

❶ 파와 피망은 다듬어 씻어놓고 피망은 길쭉길쭉 썰고 파는 통채로 끝부분만 잘라낸다. (파가 좀 굵으면 길이로 반, 가늘게 잘라 길쭉하게 한다.)

❷ 오징어는 껍질을 벗기고 깨끗이 씻어 잘게 썰어놓고 조갯살도 잘 씻어 물기를 빼고 잔새우도 잘 씻어 물기를 빼고 게맛살도 적당한 길이로 찢어놓는다.

❸ 갈아놓은 쇠고기는 볶아놓는다.

❹ ②와 ③을 합하여 후추, 볶은깨, 참기름, 소금을 넣고 섞어 조물조물 잘 버무린다.

❺ 닭국물에 달걀과 밀가루를 넣어 잘 저어둔다.

❻ 납작한 프라이팬에 식용유를 넉넉히 두르고 파와 피망을 ⑤의 반죽에 담갔다가 가지런히 놓고 ④의 양념된 해물, 쇠고기 간 것을 파 위에 골고루 놓는다. 그 위에 ⑤의 반죽을 또 뿌린다. (해물이 어스러지지 않도록)

❼ 센불에서 금방 구워야 아삭아삭하므로 밑의 파부분이 거의 다 익었을 때 뒤집는다. 뒤집기 전에 ⑤의 밀가루 반죽을 충분히 부은 다음 뒤집어야 된다.

* 보통 생선전이나 야채전은 약한 불에 부치지만, 해물전은 부칠 때 프라이팬에 기름을 넉넉히 두르고 센불에서 뜨겁게 달군 뒤 튀기듯이 지져야 바삭바삭하고 물기가 없어 맛이 있다.

🍲 4 servings

50g squid cleaned and finely chopped., 30g any shellfish, well drained and cut the same size as the squid, 50g cooked tiny shrimp, well drained, 2 imitation crab sticks, coarsely chopped, 35g lean ground beef,½ green pepper, cut into strips, 100g spring onion, cut each lengthwise into 2 halves the same length as the pepper, 1 cup chicken broth,1 cup flour, 1 egg, lightly beaten with a fork, ⅓ cup cooking oil for frying

🍲 Making

Brown the beef and let cool. Mix the seasoning ingredients together. Combine the squid, shellfish, shrimp, crab and beef and then mix in the seasonings.

Combine the chicken broth, flour and egg to make a batter. Heat oil in a skillet, dip a few pieces of spring onion and green pepper in the batter and place in the skillet over high heat. Flatten each piece slightly and, while cooking, place a little of the beef and seafood combination on top and cover with a teaspoon or so of batter. Fry until the bottom of each patty is almost cooked and crispy. Turn each one over and fry the other side very quickly until crispy. Repeat the same with the remaining pieces of onion and green pepper.

🍲 For seasoning mixture

½ tsp. black pepper, 1 tbsp. toasted sesame seeds, 1 tbsp. sesame oil, 1 tsp. salt

* Note : Pan-frying sliced fish or vegetable patties is usually done over low heat, but for this recipe, fry quickly on high heat to make patties crispy and to avoid sogginess.

해 · 물 · 요 · 리 (Seafood dishes)

국수를 곁들인 낙지볶음 (Stir-fried Octopus with Noodles)

🍲 준비는 이렇게(4인분)

낙지 1 lb., 소면 작은 3묶음(6oz.), 빨강피망 ½, 노랑피망 ½, 파 3쪽, 양파(중간크기)½, 고춧가루 1작은술, 참기름 2큰술, 후추 ½ 작은술, 볶음고추장 1½큰술, 식용유 1큰술, 다진 마늘 1큰술

🍲 만드는 것은 이렇게

먼저 낙지를 잘 씻어 먹기 좋은 크기로 썰어 물기를 뺀 다음 피망과 파, 양파등을 납작납작 썰어 양념들을 잘 혼합하여 무쳐놓고 잘 달구어진 프라이팬에 식용유를 넣고 3분간 볶은 다음 삶은 국수를 곁들여 접시에 낸다.

＊국수삶기 : 물 4컵을 냄비에 붓고 팔팔 끓을 때 소면을 골고루 넣고 잘 저은 후에 끓어오르면 찬물을 한두번 붓는다. 다 익어 국수가 위로 뜰 때 찬물에 찬 느낌이 들도록 헹구어 사리를 만들어 놓는다.

＊판판한 접시에 삶아놓은 국수사리를 돌아가면서 담고 중앙 한가운데 볶아놓은 낙지를 담아낸다.

🍲 4 servings

6 oz. thin noodles*, 4 cups water, 1 lb. small octopus*, cleaned thoroughly, cut in bite sized pieces, ½ red pepper, sliced, ½ yellow pepper, sliced, ½ medium onion, sliced, 3 spring onions, sliced, 1 tbsp. cooking oil

🍲 Making

In a pot, bring 4 cups water to a boil. While stirring, carefully add the noodles. When the noodles rise to the surface, add a ¼ cup water, and repeat this process one more time. Drain and rinse in very cold water to chill the noodles. Drain the noodles again and curl into small nest shapes for serving.

Combine the octopus with the peppers, onion and spring onion slices. Add the seasoning mixture and stir to distribute the flavors. Heat cooking oil in a heavy skillet and stir-fry the seasoned octopus for 3 minutes. Serve with the noodles side by side on the same platter.

🍲 For seasoning mix

1 tsp. hot chili powder*, 2 tbsp. sesame oil, 1½ tbsp. seasoned chili paste*, 1 tbsp. garlic, minced

＊ Available in Asian groceries.

어묵, 야채, 우동전골 (Hot Pot with Fishcake, Vegetables and Noodles)

준비는 이렇게(4인분)

오뎅 8 조각, 어묵 8 조각(½ 봉지), 시금치 5 oz, 당근 1개, 배추 ¼ 포기, 파 2뿌리, YamNoodle(곤약) 7 oz., YamCake(흰색) 6 oz., 우동국수 272g

국물 준비는 이렇게

물 6컵, 다시마(가로2인치, 세로3인치)4장, 감초뿌리 2조각, 무(작은 것) 1개, 진간장 3큰술, 정종 2큰술, 빨간 통고추 2개, 소금마늘가루(갈릭솔트) ½작은술

국물 내기

물 6 컵에 국물 재료를 넣고 15분 정도 끓여 국물을 만들고 감초뿌리, 다시마, 빨간고추, 무는 버리고 국물만 준비한다.

국수 삶기

물 8컵을 판판한 냄비에 붓고 팔팔 끓을 때 국수를 넣고 12분 정도 끓이다가 찬물에 씻어 건져 사리를 만든다.

전골 만들기

❶ 오뎅은 어떤 종류이든 상관 없이 사방 1.5인치 정도 크기로 납작납작하게 썰어서 8조각을 준비하고 나무판 위에 붙은 빨간 테의 어묵도 8조각을 납작하게 썰어두고 시금치는 물에 깨끗이 씻어 2컵의 물이 팔팔 끓을 때 시금치를 넣고 1분 정도 있다가 꺼내어 찬물에 씻은 뒤 물기를 꼭 짜놓는다.(삶아 냉동시킨 시금치를 사용해도 좋다)

❷ 당근은 껍질을 벗기고 큼직하게 채썬다. 배추는 굵직하게 채썬다.(가로 0.5인치, 세로 2.5인치)

❸ 파 2뿌리도 배추 크기로 썰고 YAM국수도 깨끗이 씻어 먹기 좋게 3등분 썰어놓고 YAMCAKE은 납작납작하게 결로 썰어 놓는다.

❹ 위의 것들이 모두 준비되면 판판한 냄비에 돌려가면서 색맞추어 놓고 먹기 전에 국물을 붓고 끓을 때 국수를 조금씩 나누어 넣어가며 계속 끓이면서 국수를 넣어가면서 먹는다.

4 servings

272 g. Japanese noodles, 7 oz. yam noodles*, cut in bite sized lengths, 1 carrot, cut in big strips, 2 spring onions, cut 1½″ long, 8 pieces odeng* (assorted fried or steamed fishcake), cut in bite sized pieces, 3-4 Napa cabbage leaves, cut in 1″ slices, 5 oz. spinach leaves, blanched one minute, gently squeezed, or frozen and thawed, 8 slices red rind fishcake (kamaboko* which comes on a wooden board), 6 oz. yamcake*, cut in bite sized pieces

Making

Combine all the broth ingredients in a saucepan and boil for 15 minutes. Strain and reserve the broth, while discarding the rest.
Cook the Japanese noodles in 8 cups boiling water about 12 minutes or until done. Rinse in cold water, drain and, while wet, shape into plum size bundles. Reheat the prepared broth.
In a shallow, preferably electric, skillet, attractively arrange all remaining ingredients, except the cooked noodles, which are served on a separate platter. Place the electric skillet on the dining table and carefully pour in the hot broth. When boiling, dip the noodles in the hot soup with the vegetables and enjoy.

For broth

6 cups water, 4 pieces dried kelp*, 2″x 3″ each, 2 slices licorice root*, 3 tbsp. dark soy sauce, 2 tbsp. sake (rice wine), 1 small radish, 1 small hot chili, ½ tsp. garlic powder, salt to taste

* Available in Asian groceries.

왕만두 전골(Stuffed Giant Dumplings)

🍜 만두피 준비는 이렇게(4인분)

밀가루 4 cup, 물 1½ 컵, 녹말가루 3큰술

🍜 만두피 만드는 것은 이렇게

❶ 밀가루에 물을 붓고 7~8분 동안 치대면서 엉겨붙게 주무른다.
❷ 반죽이 되면 8등분하고 밀가루 반죽에 녹말가루를 발라가면서 밀대에 민다.(사방 24cm정도)8장을 준비한다.

🍜 만두속 준비는 이렇게

쇠고기(간 것) ⅓ lb., 캬베츠 다진 것 1컵, 송이버섯 다진 것 1컵, 호박 다져 소금에 절임 1컵, 다진 파 1컵, 삶은 당면(다진 것) 1cup, 두부 ½모, 당근(중간크기)2개다짐, 달걀 1개, 소금(작은술) ¼, 볶은깨 2큰술, 참기름 2큰술, 후추 ¼작은술, 다진 마늘 2큰술

🍜 만두속 만드는 것은 이렇게

❶ 갈아놓은 쇠고기를 분량대로 준비한다.
❷ 호박 1개를 다져 소금(½큰술)넣고 버무린 뒤 물기를 꼭 짜놓는다.
❸ 당면(1.3oz~37.5g)은 팔팔 끓는 물에 삶아 찬물에 헹군 뒤 물기를 빼고 잘게 다진다.
❹ 두부 ½모는 타월에 싸서 꼭 짜면 물기가 빠진다.
❺ 모든 재료(캬베츠, 송이버섯, 다진 파, 당근, 달걀흰자1개)를 다 혼합, 잘 버무린 다음 양념(소금, 참기름, 볶은깨, 후추, 다진마늘)도 같이 넣고 혼합한다.
❻ 준비한 만두피에 위의 속을 꽉 채우고 노른자를 발라 꼭꼭 누르면서 오므린다.

🍜 국물 준비는 이렇게

육수국물 8컵, 다시마(가로5cm,세로8cm) 3장, 무 4쪽(사방 4cm,두께 2cm 정도), 불린 표고버섯 2장(채썬 것), 떡국떡 1컵, 소금과 마늘가루 ½작은술

🍜 국물 만드는 것은 이렇게

❶ 육수국물 8컵에 준비한 다시마, 무, 표고버섯, 소금과 마늘가루½작은술을 넣고 끓이다가 5분쯤 지난 후 무와 다시마는 건져낸다.
❷ 만들어놓은 만두를 위의 국물에 넣고 떡국떡 1컵도 함께 넣고 10분 정도 끓인 뒤 각자 접시에 왕만두 1개씩 먼저 담고 양념장을 끼얹어가면서 먹는다.
* 양념장 만들기: 진간장 ⅓ 컵, 볶은깨 1큰술, 고춧가루 1큰술, 다진생강½작은술, 정종 1큰술, 참기름 ½작은술 - 잘 섞어놓는다.

🍜 4 servings

½ tbsp. salt, 1 cup zucchini, chopped, 1 cup transparent noodles, ½ lb. bean curd, ⅓ lb. lean ground beef, 1 cup cabbage, chopped, 1 cup black mushrooms, chopped, 1 cup spring onion, chopped, 2 carrots, finely chopped, 1 egg white, 2 tbsp. sesame seeds, toasted, 2 tbsp. sesame oil, ¼ tsp. black pepper, ¼ tsp. salt, 2 tbsp. minced garlic cheesecloth for wringing bean curd

🍜 Making

Sprinkle ½ tablespoon salt on the zucchini, wait 10 minutes, then squeeze out any liquid. Cook the noodles in boiling water for 1 minute, rinse in cold water, drain and chop into bite sized pieces. Wrap bean curd in a double layer of cheesecloth and squeeze out the water. Thoroughly combine the beef, bean curd and vegetables, then add all remaining ingredients and mix well.

Make the dumpling wrap dough by mixing the flour and water. Knead for 7-8 minutes and divide into 8 pieces. Roll each piece to make a 9½″ circle and dust with cornstarch. Drop ⅛ of the filling in the center of each circle, fold in the edges and pinch to seal the filling inside and form a 4-5″size dumpling. Set aside and prepare soup. In a skillet wide enough to accommodate 4 dumplings in a single layer, bring the broth to a boil. Add the kelp, radish and mushrooms and cook for 5 minutes. Carefully drop in 4 dumplings and cook for 10 minutes over medium heat. Add ½ cup of the rice cake around the dumplings and cook for another minute.

Serve one dumpling in an individual shallow bowl with a little of the soup, leaving more than half the soup to cook the next 4 dumplings and remaining ½ cup of rice cake. (While eating, cook the other 4 dumplings.) Add seasoned soy sauce (see recipe below) to taste.

🍜 For dumpling wrap

4 cups flour, 1½ cups water, cornstarch for dusting

🍜 For soup

8 cups meat broth or any other kind, 3 pieces kelp, 2″ x 3″ each, 4 slices radish, each 1½″ x 1½″ x ¾″ thick, 2 black mushrooms, softened in water and cut into strips, 1 cup sliced rice cake, soaked in water for 30 minutes, garlic salt ½tsp.

🍜 For seasoned soy sauce, combine the following six ingredients

⅓ cup soy sauce, 1 tbsp. toasted sesame seeds, 1 tsp. hot chili powder (available in Asian grocery),½ tsp. minced ginger, 1 tsp. sake (rice wine), ½ tsp. sesame oil

국·수·국·물·요·리 (Noodle and Soups)

오색소면전골(Colorful Hot Pot with Noodles)

준비는 이렇게(3인분)

소면(가는국수) ½ lb., 소고기 700g, 양파 1개, 파 3뿌리, 오징어 ½ 마리, 새우 10마리, 불린 표고버섯 8쪽, 어묵 1개(빨강색), 달걀 3개(삶음), 쑥갓 (약간), 붉은 고추 3개(작은), 피클용 오이 1½

만드는 것은 이렇게

❶ 물 12컵에 양파 1개, 쇠고기 700g을 넣고 40~45분 정도 푹 삶아 양파는 건져버리고 고기는 건져 납작납작하게 썰고 국물은 기름을 걷고 맑은 육수를 만든다.

❷ 오징어는 껍질을 벗겨 0.5 cm 간격으로 칼집을 넣고 끓는 물에 삶아 데친 다음 길쭉길쭉 잘라놓는다.

❸ 오이는 7cm길이로 납작납작하게 썬다.

❹ 어묵은 0.5 cm두께로 어슷어슷하게 썬다.

❺ 달걀은 푹 익혀 삶아놓는다.(½로 어슷어슷 꽃모양으로 잘라놓는다)

❻ 새우는 물기를 뺀다.

❼ 붉은 고추는 어슷어슷 둥글게 썬다.

❽ 쑥갓은 잎 부분만 짧게 잘라놓는다.

❾ 불린 표고버섯은 잘 다듬어 길쭉길쭉 썰어 프라이팬에 살짝 볶아둔다.

❿ 국수는 잘 삶아 놓는다.

● 전골냄비에 보기좋게 국수사리를 먼저 4군데 놓고 편육과 데친 오징어, 새우, 오이를 옆옆이 돌려담고, 파 3뿌리는 어슷어슷 썰어 놓고 한 가운데 모양있게 어묵과 달걀을 놓고 준비해 놓은 육수를 부어 끓이다가 식사할 때 준비한 양념장을 골고루 끼얹고 간을 맞추어 불끄기 전에 쑥갓을 얹어놓는다.

● 소면전골은 특히 겨울철에 따뜻하게 해서 먹으면 더욱 좋다.

● 양념장 만들기: 진간장 ⅓ 컵, 고춧가루1큰술, 다진마늘 1큰술,
　　　　　　　　다진 파 2큰술을 모두 섞는다.

＊국수 삶는 법은 86쪽 오색냉소면 참조.

3 servings

700g beef, 1 onion, 12 cups water, ½ squid, 10 shrimp, shelled, deveined and patted dry, 1 steamed fishcake* with red outer color, diagonally sliced, 8 black mushrooms, softened in water, cut in thick strips, stir fried with a little oil, 3 fresh red chili, diagonally sliced, 1½ pickling cucumbers, cut into 3″ strips, 3 spring onions, cut into 3″ pieces,
3 eggs, boiled, cut zigzag into halves,½ lb. thin noodles*, quickly cooked in boiling water, rinsed in cold water, drained and while wet, shaped into four round nests or bundles, beef broth (see recipe) to cover the ingredients, 12 sue-kaht* leaves (edible chrysanthemum)

Making

Put the beef and onion in the water and boil a few minutes, then simmer 40-45 minutes until the beef is tender. While the broth cools, remove the beef and cut into thin, bite size slices. Skim the fat from the broth, discard the onion, and strain to yield a clear broth.

Peel and slit the squid open and lay it flat with the inside facing up. Holding a sharp knife at a 45 degree angle to the working surface, score the squid diagonally every ¼″ in a trellis pattern. Blanch the squid in boiling water and cut into strips.

Combine the seasoned soy sauce ingredients and allow the flavors to blend.

In a saucepan suitable for the table, place the eggs in the center, place half the noodle nests on one side of the saucepan and half on the opposite side, do the same with the fishcake, and arrange the remaining items colorfully around the eggs, between the noodles and fishcake. Pour in the clear broth very carefully and heat thoroughly. Sprinkle with the seasoned soy sauce and add sue-kaht* leaves to taste. Serve at once.

For seasoned soy sauce

⅓ cup soy sauce, 1 tbsp. hot chili powder*, 1 tbsp. minced garlic, 2 tbsp. spring onion, chopped

＊ Available in Asian groceries.

(국)·수·국·물·요·리 (Noodle and Soups)

해물찌개(Seafood Hot Pot, Haemul Chigae)

🍲 준비는 이렇게(6인분)

아기조개(Baby Clams) 0.5 oz., 해물 모듬 12 oz.(새우,낙지,홍합,오징어, 꼴뚜기, 둥근조개 등 합친 것), 꽃게 ½쪽, 파 2쪽, 배추줄기 2잎, 양파 1 개, 당근 썬 것 4쪽, 곤약 7oz., 불린표고버섯 1장, 떡국떡 6피스, 생우동 9oz., 갈릭솔트 ½작은술, 다진마늘 1작은술, 육수 2½컵, 조개국물(통조림 아기조개) – ⅓컵, 볶은고추장 1작은술, 정종 1작은술, 후추 ½작은술

🍲 만드는 것은 이렇게

❶ 해물모듬(새우,낙지,홍합,오징어,꼴뚜기,둥근조개 합친 것)을 깨끗이 씻어 물기를 뺀다.

❷ 꽃게 ½쪽은 잘 씻어 4등분한다. 파, 배추줄기, 양파, 당근, 불린 표고버섯은 크기를 비슷하게 길이 3인치 정도로 썰어 놓는다.

❸ 곤약은 씻어놓고 떡국떡은 물에 담갔다가 건져놓는다.

❹ 육수 2½컵과 조개국물 ⅓컵을 판판한 냄비에 붓고 다진마늘과 갈릭솔트, 후추를 분량대로 넣고 볶은고추장을 국물에 잘 풀어 한소끔 끓이다가 4등분한 꽃게를 넣고 또 한소끔 끓인 후에 해물모듬을 다 넣고 야채를 다 넣고 곤약과 떡국떡도 넣고 생우동도 넣고 한소끔 더 끓인다.

❺ 마지막으로 정종을 넣는다.

＊ 뜨거울 때 끓여가면서 식사할 때 즉석에서 먹는다.

＊ 종합해물(해물모듬)은 동양식품에서 12oz.짜리 봉지를 사면 좋다.

🍲 6 servings

1 pkg. frozen assorted seafood* (12oz. Hae-moul Moh-deum), thawed and drained, 5 oz. baby clams, ½ fresh crab (blue crab), cut in quarters, 2 spring onion, cut into 3″ long pieces, 2 Napa cabbage, cut in chunks, 1 onion, cut in thick slices, 4 carrot, cut in 3″ long pieces, 4 black mushrooms, softened in water and cut into thick strips, 7 oz. yam cake*, cut in bite sized pieces, 6 rice cake sticks (frozen), thawed in water and drained, 2½ cups meat broth, ⅓ cup clam juice, ½ tsp garlic salt, dash black pepper, ½ tsp. minced garlic, 1 tbsp. hot chili paste*, 9 oz. udong noodles* (a thick noodle) fresh, 1 tsp. rice wine

🍲 Making

In a saucepan, combine broth, clam juice, garlic salt, black pepper, garlic and chili paste and bring to a boil. Add the crab and, when boiling, add the remaining ingredients except the rice wine. Again bring to a boil and add the rice wine. Serve at once.

＊ Note : This dish can be prepared in an electric skillet at the table.

＊ Available in Asian groceries.

김치찌개 전골(Kimchi Hotpot)

🍲 준비는 이렇게(2인분)

돼지갈비 1lb, 김치포기(보통사이즈) ½, 포기, 파 3뿌리, 양파(중간 크기) ½, 불린 표고버섯 1개, 참기름 2큰술, 떡국떡 10쪽, 두부 ½모, 볶은고추장 1큰술, 다진마늘 1작은술, 후추 ½작은술, 볶은깨 1큰술, 물 ½컵

🍲 만드는 것은 이렇게

❶ 돼지갈비를 먹기 좋은 크기(3인치 정도)로 토막을 내고 볶은 고추장 1큰술, 참기름 2큰술, 후추 ½작은술, 볶은깨 1큰술에 문혀둔다.

❷ 양파는 채썰어두고 표고버섯도 큼직하게 채썰어둔다.

❸ 냄비에 양념무친 돼지고기와 양파, 표고버섯을 넣고 볶는다.

❹ 3, 4분정도 자작자작 소리나고 돼지고기가 거의 익을 때까지 볶는다.

❺ 배추김치 ½포기를 반을 잘라 반은 양념이 있는 그대로 반은 양념을 씻어버리고 손가락 둘째마디 정도로 썰어둔다.

❻ 냄비의 돼지고기가 익은 후에 김치를 넣고 물½컵 넣고 한소끔 끓이다가 떡과 두부를 넣는다.

🍲 2 servings

1 lb. pork spare ribs, cut in 3″ lengths, 2 tbsp. sesame oil, 1 tbsp. hot chili paste*, ½ tsp. black pepper, 1 tsp. minced garlic, 1 tbsp. toasted sesame seeds, 3 spring onions, cut 3″ long, ½ medium onion, sliced, 1 black mushroom, quartered, ½ medium cabbage kimchi, cut in 1½″ long pieces, ½ lb. bean curd, 10 slices rice cake, fresh or frozen, ½ cups water

🍲 Making

Combine chili paste, sesame oil, black pepper, garlic and sesame seeds and rub thoroughly into the ribs. In a preheated skillet, cook the ribs with the onion, spring onion and mushroom for 3-4 minutes, until sizzling. When cooked thoroughly, add a half of the kimchi with the seasoning on and the other half with the seasoning rinsed off. ½ cups water bring to a boil, add the rice cake and bean curd. Serve immediately.

＊Available in Asian groceries.

국·수·국·물·요·리 (Noodle and Soups)

미역국 (Seaweed Soup, Miyeokguk)

🥄 준비는 이렇게(3인분)

마른미역 2oz.(56.7g), 물 10컵, 참기름 2큰술, 소금마늘가루 1큰술, 쇠고기 ½ lb., 육수나 닭국물 5컵

🥄 만드는 것은 이렇게

❶ 마른 미역에 미지근한 물 10컵을 붓고 30분 정도 불린 다음 깨끗이 씻어 채에 받쳐 물기를 뺀다.

❷ 쇠고기는 채썰어 참기름 2큰술을 붓고 볶아 고기가 하얗게 익으면 씻어 놓은 미역을 넣고 다시 한번 볶다가 (2분 정도) 육수나 닭국물 5컵을 붓고 끓고부터 5분 뒤에 소금마늘가루 1큰술을 넣고 2분 정도 더 끓인 후 상에 낸다.

* 쇠고기 대신 북어채를 넣으면 북어미역국이 되고 조갯살, 해물 종류,굴 같은 것을 넣으면 해물미역국이 된다. (특히 북어와 해물은 산모에게 좋다)

* 미역의 분량이 같을 때 북어채는 4oz.를 물에 잘 씻어 물기를 빼고 쓰고, 조갯살은 7oz.정도를 쓰면 좋다.

🥄 3 servings

2 oz. dried seaweed*, 10 cups water, ½ lb.beef, 2 tbsp. sesame oil, 5 cups broth (meat or chicken), 1 tbsp. garlic salt

🥄 Making

Soak the dried seaweed in lukewarm water for 30 minutes, wash and drain in a colander. Hand tear the seaweed into bite sized pieces.
In a heavy pot, heat the sesame oil and brown the beef well. Add the seaweed and stir-fry for 2 minutes. Add the broth and boil 5 minutes. Season with garlic salt and boil another 2 minutes before serving.

* Note : This kind of soup is especially good for postnatal mothers.
　　　　Try using 4 oz. of dried shredded pollack or 7 oz. of clams
　　　　(fresh or canned) in proportion to the 2 oz. of dried seaweed.

* Available in Asian groceries.

육개장(Hearty Beef Soup, Yukgaejang)

🍲 준비는 이렇게(2인분)

쇠고기 ⅓ lb. 육수 3½컵, 감초뿌리 2조각, 물고비 ½컵, 숙주 ½컵, 파 3뿌리, 다진마늘 1큰술, 참기름 1½큰술, 고춧가루 ½큰술, 통마늘 3개, 당면 1.3oz/37.5g(삶은것 ½컵), 달걀 1개, 후추 ¼작은술, 불린 표고버섯 1장, 혼다시 ¼작은술, 소금마늘가루 1작은술, 물 6컵

🍲 만드는 것은 이렇게

❶ 물 6컵에 쇠고기 ⅓파운드를 넣고 감초뿌리 2조각을 넣고 30분 정도 고기가 젓가락으로 찔러 잘 들어갈 때까지 삶은 뒤 감초뿌리는 버리고 삶은 고기를 먹기 좋게 손으로 길쭉길쭉 찢어 놓고 국물에서 기름을 걷어낸다. 납작한 냄비에 참기름 1½큰술, 고춧가루 ½큰술, 다진 마늘 1큰술을 먼저 넣고 타지 않도록 볶다가 물고비, 채 썬 표고버섯, 숙주, 찢어놓은 고기를 넣고 육수를 붓는다.

❷ 파는 3등분으로 썰고 통마늘 3개를 납작납작 썰어넣고 3분 정도 팔팔 끓인다.

❸ 불끄기 전에 달걀 1개를 잘 풀어넣는다.

❹ 양념으로 소금마늘가루(갈릭솔트) 1작은술, 후추 ¼작은술, 혼다시 ¼작은술을 쓴다.

＊ 식성에 따라 삶은 당면 ½컵을 넣어도 됨.

🍲 당면 삶기

냄비에 물 1½컵을 붓고 팔팔 끓을 때 당면 1.3oz(37.5g)를 넣고 2분 정도 삶은 후에 찬물에 헹구어 먹기 좋은 크기로 잘라 국에 넣는다.

🍲 2 servings

2 servings ⅓ lb. Beef, 3½ cups beef broth (see recipe), 2 slices licorice root*, ½ cup presoaked fern shoots* (moul-koh-bi), ½ cup bean sprouts, 3 green onions each cut in third, 1 tbsp. minced garlic, 1 ½ tbsp. sesame oil, ½ tbsp. hot chili powder*, 3 cloves garlic thinly sliced, ½ cup transparent noodle (optional) cooked in boiling water for 2 minutes and rinsed in cold water and drained, 1 egg, ¼ tsp. black pepper, 1 black mushroom, softened in water and cut into pieces, ¼ tsp. Hondashi* (Japanese seasoned dried fish powder for soup base), 1 tsp. garlic salt, 6 cups water

🍲 Making

In a saucepan, cook the beef in boiling water and then simmer until tender. Cool and skim off the fat. Remove the beef, reserving the broth, and hand shred the beef with the grain.

In a shallow saucepan, mix and saute the beef with the sesame oil, hot chili powder, and minced garlic. While stirring, add the fern shoots, black mushroom and bean sprouts. Add the reserved beef broth (31/2 cups), garlic slices, spring onion and noodles, and boil for 3 minutes. Swirl in the egg and immediately remove the pan from the heat. Season with garlic salt, black pepper and hondahshi.

＊ Available in Asian groceries.

국 · 수 · 국 · 물 · 요 · 리 (Noodle and Soups)

갈비탕(Beef Rib Soup, Kahl-bi Tang)

🍲 준비는 이렇게(2인분)

갈비 1¾ lb., 감초뿌리 2조각, 마늘 5쪽, 파 2뿌리, 당면 1.3oz(37.5g), 무(중간크기) ½, 불린 표고버섯 2장, 죽순 3잎(can), 달걀 2개(흰자만), 물3Ltrs., 맛소금 1작은술

🍲 만드는 것은 이렇게

❶ 토막갈비에 기름이 배어 있으므로 잘 저미며 기름을 골고루 떼어 낸다.

❷ 냄비에 갈비가 잠길 정도로 물을 붓고 한소끔 끓으면 그 물을 버린다.

❸ 갈비에 물 3리터를 다시 붓고 감초뿌리 2조각을 넣고 약 40~50분 정도 끓인 뒤에 식으면 냉장고에 넣어 하룻밤을 지내면 기름이 하얗게 뜬다.

❹ 기름을 걷어내고 감초뿌리도 내버린다.

❺ 갈비고기는 건져놓고 국물만 다시 끓일 때 불린 표고버섯을 10쪽 되게 굵게 채썰어 넣고 마늘 5쪽은 1쪽을 6개로 썰어 30 피스를 넣고 중간무 ½을 굵게 깍둑썰어서 넣는다.

❻ 죽순 3잎도(가로, 세로 3인치 정도) 넣는다.

❼ 끓여서 5분 정도 되면 삶아놓은 갈비고기와 파 2뿌리(4등분으로 자름: 3인치 정도)를 넣고 달걀 흰자만 잘 풀어 넣는다.

🍲 다대기

고춧가루 2큰술, 다진파 ⅓컵, 육수 2큰술

✳ 식성에 따라 노른자를 프라이팬에 구워 지단을 만들어 국위에 얹어도 된다.

✳ 다대기(양념)를 넣어 먹어도 좋다. (화학조미료나 다시다를 넣지 않았음)

✳ 잘된 갈비탕은 뼈와 같이 살이 붙어 있으면서 아주 연해야 됨.

🍲 2 servings

1¾ lb. beef ribs, trimmed of fat, cut 2″ long, 1 medium onion, halved, 2 slices licorice root*, 2 black mushrooms, softened in water and cut into 10 strips, ½ medium radish, cut into thick strips, 3 pieces bamboo shoots*, cut into 1 inch cubes, 5 cloves garlic, sliced into 30 pieces, 1.3 oz. transparent noodles (37.5g), boiled, rinsed and drained, 2 spring onions, cut 3″ long pieces, 2 egg whites (see notes below), water for 3 liters boiling and rinsing, 1tsp. salt

🍲 Making

Place trimmed ribs in a large stockpot with onion and enough water to cover and bring to a boil. Discard water and onion. Add 3 liters of water and licorice and bring to a boil, then simmer for 40-50 minutes. Remove pot from heat, cool and refrigerate overnight.

The following day, remove any solidified fat and discard the licorice. Reheat to liquefy the broth. Remove the ribs. To the broth, add the black mushrooms, radish, bamboo shoots and garlic slices and cook for 5 minutes. Return the ribs to the broth and add the noodles and spring onions. Before serving, swirl in the lightly beaten egg whites.

✳ Note : Egg yolks can be cooked and made into strips for use as agarnish. To make the dish spicy, add a special seasoned mixture of 2 tablespoons hot chili powder, 2 table spoons broth and ⅓ cup chopped spring onions. (No MSG or Shellfish Broth Mix is included in this recipe. Perfect rib soup is when the meat is very tender, yet clings to the bone.

✳ Available in Asian groceries.

대구매운탕(Hot Spicy Cod Fish Casserole)

😋 준비는 이렇게(2인분)

대구(2 inch정도 크기) 4토막, 팽이버섯(Golden Mushrooms)- 7 oz can (통조림), 물 3컵, 감초뿌리(작고 얇은 것) 1조각, 배추줄기잎 3잎 정도 (채썰어 1컵), 무(중간크기) ¼(납작납작하게 썲음), 불린 표고버섯 2개, 파 2뿌리, 달걀 1개, 두부 5쪽 (납작납작하게 썲음)

😋 만드는 것은 이렇게

❶ 물 3컵과 감초뿌리 1조각을 넣고 2분 정도 팔팔 끓인 뒤 감초는 걷어낸다.

❷ 납작납작하게 썬 무와 물에 불린 표고버섯 (꼭지를 떼고 채썬 것)을 넣고 팔팔 끓을 때 다진마늘을 넣고 2분정도 끓인 뒤 다른 양념을 분량대로 넣고 고추장도 잘 풀어 넣는다. 거기에 배추와 팽이버섯, 대구토막을 넣고 3분 정도 팔팔 끓인 뒤 납작 납작하게 썬 두부 5쪽과 어슷어슷하게 썬 파, 달걀 1개를 풀어 위에 끼얹는다.

😋 양념 준비는 이렇게

고추장 1큰술, 다진마늘 1큰술, 후추 ¼작은술, 소금마늘가루 1작은술

😋 2 servings

4 pieces codfish, each 2″ long, 3 cups water, 1 slice licorice root, 1 medium radish, cut into bite sized slices, 1 black mushroom, softened in water, cut in strips, 1 tbsp. minced garlic, 1 tbsp. hot chili paste*, ¼ tsp.black pepper, 1 tsp. garlic salt, 1 cup Napa cabbage (about 3 leaves), cut in strips, 7 oz. golden mushrooms* (from a can), drained, 5 pieces bean curd, bite sized, 2 spring onions, cut in 2″ lengths, 1 egg, beaten lightly with a fork

😋 Making

In a saucepan, boil the water with the licorice for about 2 minutes, then discard the licorice. Add the radish and black mushroom and bring to a boil, then add the minced garlic, hot chili paste, black pepper and garlic salt and boil for 2 more minutes. Add the cabbage, canned mushrooms and codfish and boil 3 more minutes. Add the bean curd and spring onions. Finish by pouring the beaten egg over the dish like a blanket.

＊ Available in Asian groceries.

국 · 수 · 국 · 물 · 요 · 리 (Noodle and Soups)

대구탕국 (Codfish Soup, Dai-kou Tang Guk)

🍲 준비는 이렇게(3인분)

물 3 Ltr., 대구(머리포함) 5 Pcs., 두부 1모(깍두기형으로 썰음), 무 중간크기 1개(크게 썰음), 불린 표고버섯 5개(큼직큼직하게 썰음)

🍲 만드는 것은 이렇게

판판한 냄비에 물 3리터를 넣고, 큼직큼직하게 썬 무와 물에 불린 표고버섯 꼭지를 떼고 큼직큼직하게 썰어 넣고 팔팔 끓이다가 생선도 넣고 양념도 분량대로 넣고 끓이다가 배추, 파, 두부도 깍뚝형으로 썰어넣고 5분 정도 팔팔 더 끓인다.

🍲 양념 준비는 이렇게

후추 ½작은술, 마늘 큰 것 3개(납작납작하게 썬다), 소금마늘가루 1 ½ 작은술, 배추 (중간크기) ½ 포기, 파 2뿌리

* 약간 맵게 하려면 마른 빨간 고추 2개를 통째로 넣는다.

🍲 3 servings

5 pieces codfish, including fish head, with gills and innards removed, 3 liters water, 1 medium radish, cut in large slices, 5 black mushrooms, softened in water, cut in large slices, ½ tsp. black pepper, 3 cloves garlic, minced, ½ medium Napa cabbage, 2 spring onions, cut in 2″ pieces, 1 piece bean curd, cut in ¾″ cubes

🍲 Making

In a large saucepan, boil the water with the radish and black mushrooms. Add the black pepper and garlic, then the codfish pieces, including the head. A bit later, add the cabbage, spring onions and bean curd, and boil another 5 minutes.

＊ Note : To make the dish spicy hot, add 2 whole dry red chilies.

낙지, 버섯, 새우쌈요리(Lettuce Wrapped Seafood)

🦑 준비는 이렇게 (4인분)

낙지 1.5 lbs.(21 oz), 삶은새우 1 lb., 양장피 2장(삶은것 1컵), 파 5뿌리 (다진것 1컵), 당면 1.3oz(삶은당면 ½컵), 불린 표고버섯 3쪽, 싸리버섯 (통조림) ½컵, 팽이버섯 ½컵, 양파 중간크기 ½개, 상추 15장, 깻잎 15장, 쑥갓 20장, 유부초밥 10개, 주먹밥 5개, 식용유 3큰술

🦑 만드는 것은 이렇게

❶ 낙지는 깨끗이 잘 씻어 머리를 칼로 반을 갈라 골통을 떼어내고 먹기좋은 크기(2인치 정도)로 썰어 물기를 빼놓는다.

❷ 삶은 새우는 껍질이 있으면 껍질을 벗겨 깨끗이 준비한다.

❸ 양장피 2장은 2컵의 물이 팔팔 끓을 때 넣어 끓인 그대로 그 냄비에 10분 이상 두었다가 찬물에 헹군 뒤 먹기 좋게 찢어둔다.(1컵 되게 준비함)

❹ 파 5뿌리는 잘게 썰어놓는다.(1컵)

❺ 당면 1.3oz는 물 2컵이 팔팔 끓을 때 넣어 2분 정도 삶아 찬물에 씻어 먹기 좋은 크기(3인치 정도)로 잘라 놓는다.

❻ 표고버섯은 3시간 이상 물에 불린 다음 꼭지를 떼고 채썰어 놓는다.

❼ 통조림 싸리버섯은 물기를 없애고 꼭 짜둔다.

❽ 팽이버섯도 물기를 없애고 잘 씻어 놓는다.

❾ 양파는 껍질을 벗기고 반을 반달로 썰어둔다.

🦑 양념 준비는 이렇게

진간장 1큰술, 참기름 2큰술, 후추 ¼작은술, 고춧가루 1큰술, 볶은고추장 1큰술, 설탕 1큰술, 다진마늘 1큰술, 볶은깨 1큰술, 정종 1큰술

＊ 모두 합해 골고루 섞는다.

○ 상추 15장은 적당한 크기로 맞추어 잘 씻어 물기를 빼고 깻잎 15장도 잘 씻어 차곡차곡 차례로 놓고 물기를 뺀다. 쑥갓은 굵은 줄기는 따버리고 연한 순으로 20장 정도 다듬어 씻어 물기를 뺀다.

○ 쌀 2컵에 물 2½컵을 붓고 30분 정도 끓여 밥이 된 다음 식힌다.

○ 유부는 통조림(일본제품)을 쓰면 부드럽고 양념이 되어있으므로 편리하다. 유부의 물기를 꼭 짠 뒤 입을 벌려 식혀둔 밥을 1큰술 넣고 보자기 싸듯이 밥이 보이지 않게 싸놓는다.

○ 주먹밥은 밥 2컵에 설탕1큰술, 식초½작은술, 소금¼작은술을 넣고 섞은 후 밤알만큼 떼어 꼭꼭 눌러 가로 1인치, 세로 2인치 정도로 만들어 놓는다.

🦑 이렇게 만드세요

❶ 판판한 프라이팬에 식용유 3큰술을 넣고 자작자작 소리날 때 ①~⑨를 다 넣고 양념재료들을 잘 섞어서 넣고 센불에 3분 정도 볶는다.

❷ 다 익으면 큰 접시에 담고 준비한 상치, 깻잎, 쑥갓을 골고루 바꾸어 가면서 보쌈으로 싸먹는다.

❸ 그때 유부초밥과 주먹밥도 같이 곁들인다.

＊ 통조림버섯과 유부통조림은 동양식품에서 구입할 수 있다.

🦑 4 servings

10 seasoned fried bean curd pockets* (Japanese product in a tin), 6 cups cooked rice, at room temperature, 1 tbsp. sugar, ½ tsp. vinegar, 3 tbsp. cooking oil, 1 small onion, sliced, 1½ lbs. octopus, cleaned, innards removed, cut in bite sized pieces, 1 lb. shrimp, shelled, deveined and cooked, 2 mung bean starch sheets, softened in boiling water, rinsed, drained, hand torn in bite sized pieces (about 1 cup), 5 spring onions, chopped (about 1 cup), ½ cup transparent noodles, softened in boiling water, rinsed, drained and cut 3 inches long, 3 black mushrooms, softened in water for 3 hours then cut into strips, ½ cup straw mushrooms (from tin), drained, patted dry, ½ cup golden mushrooms (from tin) drained, patted dry, 15 soft lettuce leaves, cleaned and trimmed for easy wrapping, 15 kaht-nip* green leaves (perrila leaves), 20 sue-kaht* leaves (edible chrysanthemum leaves) green only, no stems, salt to taste

🦑 Making

Fill each bean curd pocket with a tablespoonful of rice, tucking one end into the other to form a packet. Season the leftover rice (about 2 cups) with mixture of 1 tablespoon sugar, ½ teaspoon vinegar and salt to taste. With your hands wet, shape into 4-5 rice balls.

In a skillet, heat oil until it splatters and stir-fry the small onion slices for a minute. Add the next 8 ingredients and the seasoning mixture and cook for 3 minutes on high heat.

Arrange on a serving platter and serve with lettuce leaves, two kinds of green leaves, bean curd pockets and rice balls arranged on a second platter. At the table, diners place a small portion of each on a lettuce leaf, wrap and enjoy.

🦑 For the seasoning mixture

1 tbsp. dark soy sauce, 2 tbsp. sesame oil, ¼ tsp. black pepper, 1 tbsp. hot chili powder*, 1 tbsp. hot chili paste*, 1 tbsp. minced garlic, 1 tbsp. rice wine, 1 tbsp. sugar, 1 tbsp. toasted sesame seeds

＊ Available in Asian groceries.

뚝배기 된장찌개(Traditional Bean Paste Dish)

준비는 이렇게(1인분)

된장(한국된장) 1큰술, 쇠고기(깍둑썰기형) 10피스, 풋고추 4개(깍둑썰기), 무(깍둑썰기) ⅓컵, 두부 ¼모, 양파 ½쪽(깍둑썰기), 파 3뿌리(손가락마디로 썰기), 호박(깍둑썰기)12쪽, 고춧가루 ½작은술, 다진마늘 1작은술, 멸치가루 1작은술, 참기름 ½작은술, 물 1½컵, 실고추 약간

만드는 것은 이렇게

❶ 쇠고기에 참기름을 넣고 볶다가 고춧가루와 무를 넣어 볶다가 된장을 넣고 볶는다.

❷ 고기가 익으면 물 1½컵을 붓고 양파, 풋고추, 호박 순서로 넣고 끓을 때 다진마늘과 두부를 잘게 썰어 넣고 파 3뿌리를 넣고 혼다시다나 혹은 멸치가루를 조금(1작은술)넣고 바글바글할 때 실고추를 약간 뿌려 상에 낸다.

I serving(traditionally prepared in earthenware)

3 oz. beef, diced into ½″ cubes, ½ tsp. sesame oil, ½ tsp. hot chili powder*, ⅓ cup radish, diced, 1 tbsp. Korean bean paste*, 1½ cups water, ½ onion, diced, 4 green chilies, sliced, ½ medium zucchini, diced in10-12 pieces, 1 tsp. minced garlic, ¼ lb. bean curd, diced into 10-12 pieces, 3 spring onions, cut in1½″ long pieces, 1 tsp. Shellfish Broth Mix* powder or anchovy powder, shredded red chili for garnish

Making

Brown beef in heated sesame oil. Add chili powder and radish and cook until beef is done. Add the Korean bean paste, water, onion, green chilies and zucchini and bring to a boil. Then add the garlic, bean curd, spring onions and Shellfish Broth powder. When it boils, sprinkle with shredded red chili and serve at once.

＊Available in Asian groceries.

떡국(Rice Cake Soup, Deuk-guk)

🍶 준비는 이렇게(1인분)

떡국떡 1½컵, 쇠고기 ¼ lb., 물 6컵, 소금마늘가루(갈릭솔트) ½작은술, 달걀 1개, 구운김(부스러뜨린 것) 1큰술, 황백지단 2큰술

🍶 만드는 것은 이렇게

❶ 떡국떡에 물을 잠길 정도로 붓고 3시간 이상 불린 후 물 2컵을 냄비에 붓고 팔팔 끓으면 불린 떡을 넣는다.

❷ 떡이 익으면 위로 뜬다.(2분 정도) 삶은 떡은 찬물에 헹군 뒤 국수채반 같은 얼개미에 담아 물기를 뺀다.

❸ 물 4컵을 붓고 쇠고기 ¼ lb.를 고기가 물러질 때까지 삶는다. (20분 정도 되면 고기국물이 2컵 정도 된다.)

❹ 기름을 걷고 고기는 편육으로 썰어놓는다. 위의 2컵 정도의 고깃국물에 갈릭솔트를 ½작은술 넣고 한번 더 끓인다.

❺ 삶아놓은 떡을 대접에 담고 육수를 붓고 고명(황백지단, 김, 쇠고기편육)을 위로 올리고 먹는다.

＊식성에 따라 육수국물에 달걀 1개를 풀어도 좋다.

＊쇠고기를 가늘게 채썰어 볶아 써도 됨.

＊두부 몇 쪽을 깍뚝 썰어 넣어도 됨.

🍶 I serving

1½ cups sliced rice cake*, frozen or fresh, ¼ lb. beef, in one piece, ½ tsp. garlic salt, 1 sheet toasted seaweed*, crumbled by hand, 2 tbsp. egg pancake strips (yellow and white), water, as needed

🍶 Making

Soak the rice cake in enough water to cover for 3 hours and then drain in colander. In a saucepan, boil 2 cups of water, carefully add the beef and return to a boil. Simmer the meat until tender when tested with a fork. Remove the beef and cut into thin slices. Boil the beef broth with garlic salt for a couple more minutes and keep warm.

In another pan, heat the rice cake in 2 cups boiling water for a couple of minutes and drain. To serve, put the rice cake in a bowl, pour in the broth and garnish with crumbled seaweed, beef slices and egg strips.

＊Notes : A beaten egg can be poured into the hot soup in place of the egg strips.

Ground beef or thin strips of beef, browned in a skillet with 1 tablespoon sesame oil, then cooked in 2 cups boiling water with garlic salt, can be substituted for the piece of beef and beef broth.

＊Available in Asian groceries.

만두국, 물만두국

(Stuffed Dumpling Soup, Boiled Dumplings)

🍲 준비는 이렇게 (4인분)

쇠고기(갈아둠) ½ lb., 캬베츠(중간크기) ¼등분, 호박(1개) 0.4 lb., 불린 표고버섯 1장, 두부 1모(19 oz.), 당면 2.2 oz., 만두피 1팩, 물 3큰술

🍲 만드는 것은 이렇게

❶ 갈아놓은 쇠고기를 반(½)으로 나누어 나눈 반은 볶아 익히고 나머지 반은 생고기로 쓴다.
❷ 캬베츠 ¼등분한 것을 아주 잘게 다져둔 다음 소금 ½작은술 넣고 절였다가 30분 후 물기를 꼭 짜놓는다.
❸ 호박 1개를 잘게 다져서 소금 ½작은술 넣고 절였다가 30분 후 물기를 꼭 짜 놓는다.
❹ 두부 한모(19oz.)는 얇은 보자기에 싸서 꼭꼭 짜면서 물기를 뺀다.
❺ 당면(2.2oz.)은 삶아 잘게 다진다.(1컵 정도 됨) 물에 불린 표고버섯 1장도 아주 작게 다진다.
❻ 모든 재료가 다 준비된 후에 한데 섞고 양념을 같이 넣은 다음 골고루 잘 주물러둔다.(흰자도 같이)

🍲 양념 준비는 이렇게

볶은깨 2큰술, 다진마늘 ½큰술, 다진생강 1작은술, 참기름 1작은술, 소금마늘가루 1작은술, 달걀흰자 1개

🍲 만두 만들기는 이렇게

만두피를 가지런히 놓고 달걀 노른자 1개를 물 3큰술과 섞어 만두피에 바른 뒤 준비한 속을 넣고 만두를 모양있게 빚는다.

🍲 만두 국물은 이렇게

육수국물에 소금마늘가루를 적당히 넣고 끓이다가 먹기 직전에 삶아놓은 당면을 대접에 담고 미리 따로 삶아놓은 만두를 담고 위에 고명으로 황백지단을 어슷어슷 썰어놓고 다진 파를 몇 점 놓고 편육 3, 4점을 위에 놓고 국물을 붓고 상에 낸다.

🍲 물만두는 이렇게

물만두는 그냥 물에 삶아서 만두가 위로 떠오르면 익은 것이므로 건져 내어 접시에 담아 그냥 내놓고 따로 양념장(진간장에 식초 조금)을 준비한다.

○ 만두 삶는 물의 분량은 끓는물 8컵에 만두 16개 정도 넣으면 된다.
＊식성에 따라 만두속의 야채를 변경할 수 있다. 중국사람들은 반드시 돼지고기와 부추만 쓴다. 그러나 한국사람들은 야채를 많이 씀. 표고버섯이 싫으면 양송이를 써도 됨.
＊만두를 빚어 냉동하려면 2시간쯤 밖에 두었다가 냉동시키고 냉동된 만두를 금방 삶으려면 팔팔 끓는물에 냉동만두를 넣고 위로 뜨면 찬물 1컵을 떠오른 만두솥에 붓는다. 두번 반복한다.

🍲 4 servings

½ lb. lean ground beef, 2 cups cabbage, chopped, 1 zucchini (about ½ lb.), chopped, sprinkled with salt and liquid squeezed out, 19 oz. bean curd, squeezed water out in double cheesecloth, 1 black mushroom, softened in water and chopped, 2.2 oz. transparent noodles, boiled, drained and chopped (1 cup), 2 tbsp. toasted sesame seeds, ½ tbsp. minced garlic, 1 tsp. minced ginger, 1 tsp. sesame oil, 1 tsp. garlic salt, 1 egg white, saving the yolk for sealing wrappers, 1 pkg. wonton wrappers, 3 tbsp. water

🍲 Making

Brown half of the ground beef, and then add the cabbage, zucchini, bean curd, black mushroom, transparent noodles and the remaining beef. Combine the rest of the ingredients, except wonton wrappers, and blend thoroughly into the above mixture. Place a teaspoonful of the filling mixture on each wrapper. Brush the edges with egg yolk and seal securely by gathering the edges to the middle and pinching them together. Place on dry kitchen towel dusted with flour.

🍲 For soup

8 cups broth (beef or chicken broth), 1 cup transparent noodles (optional), 2 spring onions, chopped, boiled beef (optional), 12 thin slices, garlic salt to taste, egg strips (white & yellow) garnish

🍲 soup making

Boil the broth. Cook and drain the noodles. Arrange 5-6 dumplings and some noodles in a soup bowl. Pour in the boiling broth. Season and garnish with spring onions, beef slices and egg strips to taste.
To make boiled dumplings, boil 8 cups water and carefully drop in the dumplings, up to 16 at a time. When they rise to the surface add 1 cup water and repeat once more. Remove with a slotted spoon. Serve with vinegar mixed with soy sauce.

＊Note : Vary vegetables to taste, and substitute pork or chicken for beef.
Chinese prefer pork and garlic chives for filling · Koreans like more vegetables.
Dumplings must be at room temperature for two hours before freezing. To cook frozen dumplings, add water, 1 cup at a time, at each boiling point.

해장국(Hot and Spicy Soup)

🍲 준비는 이렇게(3인분)

육수나 닭국물(8컵), 배추 ½(중간포기), 파(5뿌리), 콩나물 4oz, 풋고추 2개, 빨강고추 1개

🍲 만드는 것은 이렇게

❶ 오목하고 판판한 냄비에 육수나 닭국물(8컵)을 붓고 배추는 가로 1인치, 세로 3인치로 썰어 넣고 파도 같은 배추 사이즈로 썰어 넣고 콩나물은 깨끗이 씻어 물기를 빼고 넣고 풋고추와 빨강 통고추도 어슷어슷 3등분씩 썰어 넣는다.

❷ 된장(1큰술)은 잘 풀어 덩어리지지 않도록 풀어 국에 넣고 후추, 소금, 다진마늘, 참기름, 고추장, 고춧가루를 분량대로 넣고 끓인다. 끓을 때쯤 물(3큰술), 밀가루(1큰술)을 풀어 넣는다. 끓고부터 8~10분쯤 뒤에 상에 낸다.

🍲 양념 준비는 이렇게

(한국)된장 1큰술, 후춧가루 ¼작은술, 소금 1½작은술, 다진마늘 1큰술, 참기름 1큰술, 고추장 ½큰술, 고춧가루 ½큰술, 밀가루 1큰술, 물 3큰술

🍲 3 servings

8 cups beef or chicken stock, one-half of a medium-size cabbage, 5 spring onions, 4 oz. bean sprouts, 2 green peppers, 1 red pepper, 1tbsp. Korea bean paste, ½ small tsp. black pepper, 1 tbsp. chopped garlic, 1 tbsp. sesame oil, ½ tbsp. red pepper paste, 1tbsp. flour, 3tbsp. water.

🍲 Making

In a medium sauce pan, pour in beef or chicken stock. Cut cabbage and spring onion into small-bite size pieces and into stock. Rinse bean sprouts and drain well. Add them to the stock. Add julienned green and red peppers.

Add Korean bean paste and the rest of the seasonings except for the water and flour. Bring ingredients to a boil. When the mixture starts to boil, add water and flour and make sure it's well mixed. Boil another 8-10 minutes.

북어국(Dried Pollack Soup)

준비는 이렇게(6인분)

말린 북어 6oz(170g), 물 2 Ltrs., 불린 표고버섯 큰것 2장, 무(중간크기) 1개(1.4lbs.), 배춧잎 10장, 파 20뿌리, 참기름 1½큰술, 북어불린물 2 Ltrs.

만드는 것은 이렇게

❶ 말린 북어에 물 2리터를 붓고 3시간 이상 불려 놓는다.
❷ 북어를 물에서 건져내고 남은 물은 나중에 국물로 끓일 때 쓴다.
❸ 물에 불린 북어의 뼈를 발라내고 먹기좋은 크기(손가락 하나 크기)로 손으로 찢든지 칼로 썬다.
❹ 참기름 1½큰술을 냄비에 먼저 넣고 장만한 북어를 넣어 2분 정도 자작자작 소리날 때까지 젓다가 북어 불린 물(2리터 정도)을 붓고 물 2리터를 더 붓는다.
❺ 불린 표고버섯을 큼직큼직 채썰고(10쪽 정도) 파 흰쪽뿌리는 4인치 정도 통째로 먼저 썰어 넣고 파란 파잎은 맨 나중에 넣는다.
❻ 배추는 줄기부터 잎사귀까지 큼직하게 채썰어 넣고 무도 납작 납작 썰어넣고 끓인다.
❼ 마지막으로 양념재료들을 식성에 따라 넣는다.

양념 준비는 이렇게

후추 ½작은술, 소금마늘가루(갈릭솔트) 1½큰술, 다진마늘 2큰술, 혼다시 1작은술

6 servings

6 oz.(170g) dried pollack*, 2 liters water, 2 large black mushrooms, softened in water and cut into 10 slices, 1 radish, medium (about 1.4 lb.), sliced, 10 leaves Napa cabbage, cut in large slices, 20 springs onions, cut with green parts separated from white parts, 1½ tbsp. sesame oil

Making

Soak the dried pollack in 2 liters of water for 3 hours or longer. Remove softened fish, reserving the water to use as soup base. Remove any bones still attached to the Pollack and cut fish into bite sized pieces (thumb size). Heat the sesame oil in a saucepan, add the pollack and stir-fry for 2 minutes or until pieces sizzle. Add the reserved water, mushrooms, white parts of the spring onion, cabbage and radish. Bring to a boil and then add the green parts of the spring onion.

Combine the seasoning ingredients and present in a small serving bowl. At the table, each diner can stir in seasonings according to individual taste.

For seasoning

½ tsp. black pepper, 1½ tbsp. garlic salt, 2 tbsp. minced garlic, 1 tsp. fish broth mix*

＊Available in Asian groceries.

오색 냉소면(Five-Colors Cold Noodle)

🍲 준비는 이렇게(5~6인분)

소면(가는국수) 1lb., 양장피 4장, 달걀 2개, 삶은새우 30마리, 쑥갓
(120g) 1단, 채썬 오이 1컵, 불린 표고버섯 8개(채썰음), 무 약간(강판에
감), 파 3쪽, 구워서 부스러뜨린 김(약간), 식용유 3큰술

🍲 만드는 것은 이렇게

❶ 물8컵을 판판한 냄비에 붓고 끓어오르면 국수를 분량대로
넣고, 국수가 끓어 위로 오르면 그때 찬물을 약간 넣고 2번 내
지 3번 휘저어서 반짝반짝할 때 찬물에 3~4번 헹구어 사리를
만들어 물기를 빼놓는다.

❷ 양장피 4장은 물 5컵을 냄비에 붓고 끓을 때 넣어 뚜껑을 닫고
불을 끈 뒤에 20분 정도 그대로 두었다가 부풀어 오르면 먹기
좋은 사이즈로 찢어 놓는다.

❸ 달걀 2개는 잘 풀어 달구어진 프라이팬에 식용유 2큰술을 붓
고 판판하게 지단을 부치고 식은 후 채썰어 놓는다.

❹ 삶은 새우는 껍질이 있으면 까놓고 물기를 뺀다.

❺ 쑥갓은 잘 씻어 잎사귀만 물기를 뺀다. 오이(피클) 2개 정도는
잘 씻어 채썰어 놓는다.

❻ 3시간 이상 불린 표고버섯은 기둥을 떼고 잘 씻어 채썰어
프라이팬에 식용유1큰술을 넣고 볶아 놓는다.

❼ 무(중간) ¼쪽은 강판에 갈고 파는 잘게 다져놓고 김은 3장
정도 구워서 부셔놓는다.

🍲 국물 맛내기

물 6컵, 다시마(사방 10cm 크기) 3장, 생선소스(Fish Sauce 3큰술),
포도주 1½큰술을 혼합하여 팔팔 끓여 식히고 다시마는 버린다.

🍲 상차림은 이렇게

넓은 접시에 삶아 놓은 국수를 담고, 양장피도 사이사이에 놓고
국수사리 위에 ❸~❻을 보기좋게 올린다. 준비한 다시마 국물은
1인분씩 나누어 그릇에 담고 무즙, 다진파, 구운김을 곁들인다.
국수사리를 한 뭉치씩 국물에 담갔다가 건져먹는다.

＊ 식성에 따라 와사비, 갖은 양념장을(국수양념장)을 쓰기도 한다.
  (와사비 1큰술, 물 1½큰술 같이 혼합)

＊ 야채로 빨강피망이나, 노랑피망을 쓰면 향기가 좋고 맛을 더한다.

＊ Fish Sauce는 동양식품점에서, 와사비도 동양식품점에서 구입한다.

🍲 5~6 servings

4 mungbean starch sheets, 2 eggs, 1 lb. thin noodles (soh-myun)*, 30 cooked shrimp, 120g edible chrysanthemum leaves* (sue-kaht), leaves only, no stems, 1 cup cucumber, cut in fine strips, 8 black mushrooms, cut in thin strips, 3 spring onions, chopped, water, grated radish and toasted seaweed for garnish, 3 tbsp. cooking oil

🍲 Making

Cook the mungbean starch sheets in boiling water, remove from the heat and leave in the water 10 minutes or until they swell up. Drain, rinse immediately in cold water and hand tear into bite sized pieces.
Beat the eggs lightly with a fork and pour into a heated, greased skillet, tilting the pan around to spread the egg evenly and make a very thin pancake. Turn the egg over, cook for a few more seconds and cut into fine strips.
Combine all the dipping sauce ingredients and bring to a boil. Let cool. Serve sauce in individual dipping bowls.
Cook the noodles in boiling water. When they rise to the surface, add 1/4 cup cold water, bring to a boil and repeat the process one more time. Drain and rinse the noodles in cold water to chill and shape them into small bundles or nests.
Spread the mungbean on a serving platter and colorfully arrange the noodles, shrimp, mushrooms, egg strips, cucumbers and chrysanthemum leaves (sue-kuht) on top. At the table, diners may serve themselves from the platter and dip their selections into their individual bowl of sauce. Diners may add grated radish, toasted seaweed, wasabi and/or spicy seasoned soy sauce to their dipping sauce to taste.

🍲 For dipping sauce

6 cups water, 3 pieces kelp (each 4″ x 4″), 3 tbsp. fish sauce*, 1½ tbsp. wine

＊Available in Asian groceries.

국 · 수 · 국 · 물 · 요 · 리 (Noodle and Soups)

자장면(Noodles with Black Bean Sauce, Cha Chang Myun)

🍲 준비는 이렇게(6인분)

자장소스 2 컵, 감자 중간크기 5개, 당근 큰 것 1개, 양파(중간크기) 4개, 다진 쇠고기 ½ 컵, 마늘 2큰술, 참기름 3큰술, 설탕 1큰술, 조미술 1작은술, 녹말가루 4큰술, 물 ½ 컵, 자장국수 3 lbs.(48 oz), 물 6컵

🍲 만드는 것은 이렇게

❶ 자장소스 2 컵을 냄비에 담고 다진마늘 2큰술, 참기름 2큰술, 설탕 1큰술을 넣고 2분 정도 볶는다.

❷ 감자, 당근, 양파는 각각 4각형으로 썰고 다진 쇠고기 ½컵을 볶아놓은 자장에 한데 모두 혼합하고 물 6컵을 넣고 팔팔 끓인 뒤 물에 갠 녹말가루 앙금을 조금씩 부어가며 걸쭉하게 되면 잘 저어 삶아놓은 국수 위에 끼얹는다.

＊국수 삶기: 물 3 리터를 붓고 팔팔 끓을 때 국수를 넣는다. 국수가 끓어오르면 찬물을 조금씩 2~3번 붓고 2분 정도 더 끓이다가 찬물에 찬 느낌이 들도록 씻어 헹구어 놓는다. 소스를 얹기 전에 국수를 뜨거운 물에 잠깐 담갔다가 접시에 담고 소스를 얹는다.

🍲 6 servings

2 cups prepared black bean sauce*, 2 tbsp. minced garlic, 3 tbsp. sesame oil, 1 tbsp. sugar, 6 cups water, 5 medium potatoes, peeled, diced in $\frac{1}{4}''$ cubes, 1 carrot, peeled, diced in $\frac{1}{4}''$ pieces, 4 medium onions, diced $\frac{1}{4}''$, $\frac{1}{2}$ cup ground beef, 4 tbsp. cornstarch with $\frac{1}{2}$cups water, 3 lbs. thick noodles (udong noodles)*, (dry or fresh), water

🍲 Making

To complete the black bean sauce(called "cha chang myun"), combine the prepared black bean sauce, minced garlic, sesame oil and sugar and boil in a saucepan for 2-3 minutes. Add 6 cups of water, the potatoes, carrots, onions and beef, bring to a boil and then thicken with the cornstarch and water mixture.

To prepare the noodles, boil 3 liters of water in a large pot and add the noodles carefully to prevent them from sticking together. When the water again boils and noodles rise to the surface, add $\frac{1}{2}$ cup cold water, and repeat this process 2 more times. Drain and quickly rinse the noodles in cold water to cool thoroughly.

To serve, dip the noodles in boiling water to reheat, divide them in 4 individual serving bowls and pour completed "Cha-chang-myun" sauce over the noodles in each bowl.

＊ Available in Asian groceries.

짬뽕(Special Combination Noodle Soup, Cham-pong)

🍲 준비는 이렇게(4인분)

당근 중간크기 1개, 파 1단, 게살 3 oz, 표고버섯(불린 것) 4장, 쇠고기나 돼지고기(편육 10피스), 달걀 1개, 배추줄기 4장, 캬베츠 채 썬 것 1컵, 유부 3장, 새우(중간크기) 15 pcs.

🍲 만드는 것은 이렇게

❶ 양념재료의 참기름, 다진마늘, 고춧가루를 먼저 달구어놓은 냄비에 붓고 볶다가 (새우, 게살을 빼고) 버섯과 야채(당근, 파, 표고버섯, 배추줄기, 캬베츠, 유부) 모두 굵게 채썰어 넣고 30초 정도 더 볶는다.

❷ 육수국물이나 닭국물 10 컵과 편육 10쪽을 넣고 팔팔 끓인 다음 새우와 게살을 넣고 잘 풀어놓은 달걀을 넣고 3분 정도 더 끓인다.

＊아주 매운 것을 원할 때는 매운 풋고추 1개를 굵직굵직하게 썰어 야채볶을 때 넣음.

🍲 양념 준비는 이렇게

참기름 2큰술, 다진마늘 1큰술, 고춧가루 ½큰술, 소금 1큰술, 후추½ 작은술

🍲 국수 삶기

자장면의 국수삶기와 같은 방법으로 한다.
＊편육은 쇠고기나 돼지고기 삶은 것을 말한다.

🍲 4 servings

3 lb. thick noodles, dry or fresh*, 2 tbsp. sesame oil, 1 tbsp. garlic, minced, ½ tbsp. red chili powder*, 1 tbsp. salt, ½ tsp. black pepper, 4 Chinese cabbage leaves, cut ¼″, 1 cup shredded round cabbage, 1 medium size carrot, cut into strips, 6 spring onions, cut in 2″ strips, 4 dried black mushrooms, softened in warm water, cut in strips, 10 slices beef or pork, cooked and sliced thinly, 3 fried bean curd*, cut into strips, 10 cups stock (beef, pork or chicken), 3 oz. crabsticks, 15 shrimp, shelled, cleaned and deveined, 1 egg, beaten gently with a fork

🍲 Making

Boil 3 liters of water in a large pot and add the noodles carefully to prevent them from sticking together. When the water again boils and noodles rise to the surface, add ½ cup cold water, and repeat this process 2 more times. Drain and quickly rinse the noodles in cold water to cool thoroughly.

Put the sesame oil, garlic, red chili powder, salt and pepper in a heated skillet. Add both kinds of cabbage, the carrot, spring onions, mushrooms, fried bean curd and cook about 30 seconds. Add the stock and bring to a boil. Add the meat slices, shrimp and crabsticks, then gently stir in the beaten egg.

To serve, place an equal amount of noodles in each of 4 individual bowls. Cover the noodles with soup.

＊ Available in Asian groceries.

국 · 수 · 국 · 물 · 요 · 리 (Noodle and Soups)

비빔냉면(Buckwheat Noodles)

🍲 준비는 이렇게(5인분)

얼린 냉면 3봉지(1 lb×3), 물 3리터, 쇠고기 ½ lb., 다진생강 ⅓작은술, 후추 ¼작은술, 진간장 ⅓컵, 다진마늘 1작은술, 흑설탕 2큰술, 육수 2컵, 파 3뿌리(다진파 1컵), 볶은고추장 3큰술, 볶은깨 2큰술, 참기름 6큰술, 오이(피클용)3개, 배 ½쪽, 잣 1작은술

🍲 만드는 것은 이렇게

❶ 물 3리터를 냄비에 붓고 팔팔 끓을 때 얼린 냉면 3봉지를 넣고 잘 젓는다.

❷ 4분쯤 지난 뒤 찬물에 헹구어 5개의 사리를 만들어 놓는다.

❸ 쇠고기는 가늘게 채썰어 볶아놓고 볶은 국물에 생강과 마늘, 후추, 간장을 넣고 육수 2컵을 넣어서 팔팔 끓여 식혀둔 다음, 식은 국물에 흑설탕 2큰술, 다진파 1컵 정도, 고추장 3큰술, 참기름 3큰술, 볶은통깨 2큰술을 넣고 잘 젓는다.

❹ 배와 오이는 채썰어 놓는다.

❺ 먹기 직전에 삶아놓은 냉면사리를 판판한 그릇에 담고 양념 육수를 국수에 붓고 잘 버무린 다음 채썰어 놓은 오이와 배를 함께 비빈다.

❻ 참기름 3큰술 정도 더 넣어 반질반질하고 고소하게 한다.

❼ 상에 낼 때 잣을 뿌리고 삶은 달걀을 반으로 잘라 올리든지 기호에 따라 달걀지단을 채썰어 얹는다.

🍲 5 servings

½ lb. beef, cut into fine strips, ¼ tsp. black pepper, ⅓ tsp. grated ginger, ⅓ cup soy sauce, 1 tsp. minced garlic, 2 cups broth, 2 tbsp. brown sugar, 1 cup spring onions, chopped, 3 tbsp. seasoned hot chili paste, 2 tbsp. toasted sesame seeds, 6 tbsp. sesame oil, 3 lbs. frozen buckwheat noodles (1 lb. per package), 3 liters water, 3 pickling cucumbers, cut into thin strips, ½ pear, cut into thin strips, 1 tsp. pine nuts, fried egg strips for garnish

🍲 Making

In a skillet, brown the beef. Sprinkle in the black pepper and add the ginger, garlic, soy sauce and broth and bring to a vigorous boil. Let cool. Add the brown sugar, spring onions, chili paste, 3 tablespoons of sesame oil and the sesame seeds to the cooled broth.

In a large stockpot, boil the water, add the buckwheat noodles and cook for about 4 minutes. Rinse immediately in very cold water, drain and shape into 5 bundles or nests. To serve, put one bundle of noodles in each bowl, cover with broth and colorfully arrange the beef, cucumber and pear strips. Drizzle a little sesame oil over and garnish with pine nuts and egg strips to taste.

＊Available in Asian groceries.

국 · 수 · 국 · 물 · 요 · 리 (Noodle and Soups)

물냉면(Buckwheat Noodle Soup)

준비는 이렇게(4인분)

물냉면(냉동,1lb.) 3봉지, 쇠고기 1½ lbs., 감초뿌리 8조각, 육수 4½컵, 동치미 국물 4 컵, 감식초 2큰술, 배 12쪽(납작하게 썬 것), 오이 12쪽(타원형 썰기), 동치미 무 12쪽(납작하게 썸), 삶은 달걀 4 pcs., 물 6½컵, 소금 ½작은술

만드는 것은 이렇게

❶ 쇠고기는 감초뿌리를 넣고 물 6½컵을 붓고 15분 정도 센불에 끓인다.
❷ 고기가 익었는지 젓가락으로 찔러본다.
❸ 고기가 연하게 다 익으면 솥째 냉장고에 하룻밤을 넣어둔다.
❹ 하루뒤에 하얗게 뜬 기름을 말끔히 건어낸다.
❺ 감초뿌리도 버린다.
❻ 육수 4½컵에 동치미 국물 4컵 비율로 혼합한 다음 소금과 감식초를 넣는다.
❼ 삶아 건져놓은 냉면을 대접에 먼저담고 납작납작 썬 쇠고기 편육과 배, 오이, 동치미무, 삶은 달걀을 모양있게 차례로 얹고 먹기 전에 만들어 놓은 육수를 붓는다.
❽ 잣을 3,4개 띄운다.

냉면 삶는 법

❶ 물 2½ 리터를 냄비에 넣고 팔팔 끓을 때 물냉면 냉동 3봉지를 넣는다.
❷ 1분 정도 되면 덩어리가 완전히 풀어져 색이 연해지면서 삶아진다.
❸ 잘 휘저어 찬물에 빨리빨리 주무르면서 찬 느낌이 있을 때까지 씻은 뒤에 채반에 사리를 만들어 둔다.
  ＊식성에 따라 식초나 다대기 양념(고춧가루 1큰술, 육수 2큰술 혼합)을 넣고 물겨자도 첨가한다.
  ＊동치미 담는 법은 p.105 참조.
  ＊식성에 따라 소금을 더 첨가해도 됨.

4 servings (usually served cold or at room temperature)

3lb. buckwheat noodles*, frozen, 1½ lbs. beef, 8 slices licorice root*, 4 cups juice from mild radish kimchi*, 4½ cups beef broth (see recipe), 2 tbsp. seasoned vinegar*, 12 slices pear, preferably Asian pear, 12 slices cucumber (circular slices), 12 slices mild radish kimchi*, 2 boiled eggs, cut zigzag in half, water for cooking and rinsing, pine nuts for garnish, hot mustard oil* if desired

Making

In a large pot, boil 2½ liters of water and add the still frozen buckwheat noodles. After a minute or so, the noodles will separate and slowly become transparent which indicates they are done. Rinse immediately to chill, drain and, while still wet, shape into 4 round bundles or nests.

In a saucepan, bring 6½ cups water to boil, add the beef and licorice root, cook over high heat for 15 minutes or until meat is tender when tested with a fork. Let cool in the same saucepan and place it in the refrigerator.

The next day or when cold, skim off the solidified fat and remove the beef, reserving the broth. Cut the beef into thin slices. In a big bowl, combine 4½ cups beef broth, the juice from the mild radish kimchi and the vinegar to make a soup.

Place the noodles nests in individual bowls and attractively arrange the slices of beef, pear, cucumber and radish kimchi on the top. Carefully pour some soup into each bowl and garnish with egg halves and pine nuts.

＊Note : Serve vinegar or hot mustard oil on the side to suit individual tastes.
＊Available in Asian groceries.

국·수·국·물·요·리 (Noodle and Soups)

콩국(콩국수)(Creamy Soy Bean Soup)

🍲 준비는 이렇게(4인분)

메주콩 1컵, 물 6컵, 잣 ⅓컵, 소금 1작은술, 국수(소면) 1 lb.

🍲 만드는 것은 이렇게

❶ 메주콩을 잘 씻어 하룻동안 콩 1컵에 물 3컵을 붓고 불린다.
❷ 불린 콩과 물을 그대로 끓일 때 잣 ⅓컵을 함께 넣고 팔팔 끓인다. 식힌 다음 믹서기에 모두 넣어 갈아 채에 거른다.
❸ 남은 건더기 1½컵에 물 2컵을 넣고 두세번 놓아서 믹서에 곱게 간다.
❹ 채에 다시 거른 뒤 남은 건더기 1½컵에 물 1컵을 넣고 한번에 믹서에 간다.
❺ 식성에 따라 먹기 전에 각자가 소금을 조금 넣어 먹으면 한결 구수하다.
❻ 찌꺼기는 콩비지로 사용해도 된다. 김치와 고추장, 된장, 파 등을 적당히 넣고 함께 끓이면 맛이 일품이다.
* 한여름철에 소면을 삶아 콩국에 말면 콩국수가 된다. 국수 위에 고명으로 토마토 1피스, 삶은 쇠고기 편육 2피스, 지단 약간을 곁들인다.

🍲 국수 삶기

냄비에 물 2리터정도 넣고 팔팔 끓을 때 소면 국수를 넣는다. 잘 휘저어 국수가 떠오르면 몇번 더 저은 뒤에 불을 끄고 찬물에 몇번 헹구어 물기를 뺀 다음 사리를 만든다.

🍲 4 servings

1 cup soybeans, 6 cups water, ⅓cup pine nuts, 1 tsp. salt or to taste, 1 lb.noodle

🍲 Making

Wash the soybeans and soak in 5 cups water overnight. The next day, add pine nuts and cook until mushy. Remove from heat and let cool.
In a food processor blend to a thick consistency. Line a colander with a double layer of cheesecloth and set it over a large sauce pan. Pour the blended mixture in the colander and strain the liquid into the pan. Add 1 cup of water to the residue in the cheesecloth, gather the cheesecloth and squeeze, again straining all the liquid into the pan. Discard the soybean residue (or see note below) in the cheesecloth.
At the table, diners season their own serving with salt, which will bring out the nutty flavor of the beans.

*Note : In summer, add cold cooked noodles to make a flavorful noodle soup. Garnish with a slice of tomato, a couple slices of beef and fried egg strips.
Soybean residue makes a delicious dish when cooked with kimchi, chili paste, bean paste and spring onions, etc. as preferred.
To cook noodles, boil water (1½ quarts per pound) in a large pot and carefully add the noodles. When water boils and noodles rise to the surface, add ½ cup cold water.
Repeat the process twice more. Drain and rinse in cold water to stop further cooking. While wet, shape the noodles into egg-size bundles or nests for serving.

국·수·국·물·요·리 (Noodle and Soups)

소면장국수(Thin Noodle Soup with Spicy Sauce)

🍲 준비는 이렇게(4인분)

소면국수 12oz(340g), 물 8컵(64 oz.), 작은호박 1개, 달걀 2개, 식용유 1
큰술, 쇠고기 볶은 것 ½컵, 오이(씨없는 것) ½, 구워 부스러뜨린
김 ⅓컵

🍲 국수 삶기

❶ 소면 국수를 8컵(64oz.)의 물이 팔팔 끓을 때 넣어 젓가락으로
잘 저으면서 서서 지킨다. (팔팔 끓어 넘쳐오르기 때문)
❷ 2분 정도 끓고나면 국수채에 받쳐서 찬물에 헹구어낸 다음
사리를 만들어 물기를 뺀다.

🍲 국물 만들기

물 8컵(64 oz.)에 다시마와 소금마늘가루(갈릭솔트), 무, 정종,
진간장을 넣고 끓고부터 5분 정도 후에 불을 끈다. (무는 건져버림)

🍲 국수위의 고명만들기

❶ 호박은 채썰어 소금 ½작은술과 물 1컵에 팔팔 끓으면 데쳐서
차게 씻은 후 물기를 빼고 볶은깨 1큰술, 소금 ½작은술 넣고
무쳐 둔다.
❷ 지단을 황백으로 갈라 프라이팬에 부친다. (달걀을 황, 백으로
각각 풀어 잘 저은 다음 기름을 약간 두르고 납작하게 부침.)
지단을 채썰어 놓는다.
❸ 깨끗이 씻은 오이는 껍질째 채썰어놓고 기름없는 쇠고기는
채썰어서 간장 1큰술을 넣고 볶아놓는다.
❹ 김은 불에 구워 부스러뜨린다.
❺ 국수를 대접에 담고 위의 ①②③④를 색맞추어 얹어 담은
뒤 만들어 놓은 국물을 붓고 양념장은 맛을 보아가며 넣는다.

🍲 국물은 이렇게

물 8컵(64oz.), 다시마 1장 –(가로 3인치,세로 10인치), 소금마늘가루
(갈릭솔트) ⅔큰술, 무 2쪽 –(가로 2인치,세로 4인치정도), 정종 2큰술,
진간장 1큰술

🍲 양념장은 이렇게

진간장 ⅓컵, 참기름 ½작은술, 고춧가루 1큰술, 볶은깨 1큰술, 풋고
추 2개, 파 2뿌리

* 양념장을 만들 때 참기름을 너무 많이 넣으면 미끄럽고
시원한 맛이 없다.
* 식성에 따라 국물에 있는 다시마를 채썰
어 먹어도 됨.
* 풋고추와 파를 잘게 다져 재료
들을 함께 섞어 쓴다.

🍲 4 servings

1 zucchini, cut into thin strips, 1 tsp. toasted sesame seeds, ½ tsp. salt, 1 cup water to cook zucchini, 2 eggs, 1 tbsp. frying oil for eggs, ½ cucumber, unpeeled, cut in thin strips, ½ cup lean beef, cut in thin strips, 1 tbsp. soy sauce, 12 oz. thin noodles, ⅓cup toasted and crumbled seaweed, water as needed

🍲 Making

Blanch the zucchini quickly in 1 cup of salted water, then rinse in cold water. Drain thoroughly and mix with the sesame seeds and salt. Separate the egg yolks and whites and beat each lightly with a fork. Heat oil in a frying pan. Make a thin yellow and a thin white pancake, tilting the pan to spread the egg evenly. Cut each pancake in thin strips. Stir stir-fry the beef with 1 tablespoon soy sauce. In a pot, bring 8 cups of water to boil and cook the noodles, stirring until the water boils, about 2 minutes. Drain the noodles, rinse in cold water and shape them in 4 nests or round bundles.
Combining the listed broth ingredients and boil for 5 minutes. Discard the radish and reserve the kelp for later use. Combine the seasoned soy sauce ingredients. Place noodles in 4 individual bowls and arrange the prepared items on top. Carefully pour in the hot broth. Serve the seasoned soy sauce on the side to be added to personal taste and garnish with toasted seaweed.

🍲 For broth

8 cups water, 1 kelp sheet, 3″ x 10″, ⅔ tbsp. garlic salt, 2 radishes, each 2″ x 4″, 2 tbsp. rice wine, 1 tbsp. soy sauce

🍲 For seasoned soy

⅓cup soy sauce, 2 springs onions, chopped, 1 tbsp. hot chili powder, 2 green chilies, chopped, ½ tsp. sesame oil, 1 tbsp. toasted sesame seeds

Note : Too much sesame oil in the seasoned soy will decrease the
freshness of the flavor.
Kelp from the broth can be cut into thin strips and used as a
topping for this soup.

같은 소스로 10가지이상
마른반찬 만들기(Basic Sauce for Side Dishes)

🍲 소스 만들기

생강물 3컵(납작하게 썬 생강 35쪽과 물 5컵을 넣고 3컵이 되도록 조림), 간장 2컵, 마늘 10쪽, Fish Sauce ½ 컵, 물엿 ⅓ 컵, 브라운설탕 6큰술, 포도주 2큰술, 모두를 잘 섞어 35~50분 동안 센불에 조린다.

🍲 만드는 것은 이렇게

판판한 프라이팬에 아래의 재료별로 명시된 분량의 소스를 먼저 넣고 바글바글 끓을 때 양념과 재료를 넣고 1~2분 정도 볶아낸다.

- 🌀 **무 말랭이** : 5시간 이상 물에 불린 무말랭이 – 깨끗이 씻어 물기 뺀 것 2½컵 , 소스 1½큰술, 볶은고추장 ½큰술, 고춧가루 1작은술, 볶은깨 1큰술, 설탕 1큰술, 참기름 1큰술

- 🌀 **김과 물고비** : 김 10장(구어서 부스러뜨림), 깨끗이 씻은 물고비 1½ 컵(잘게 썰음), 볶은깨 1큰술, 참기름 1큰술, 소스 2½큰술

- 🌀 **오징어 채** : 오징어채 4oz(113g), 소스 2½큰술, 참기름 1큰술, 볶은깨 1큰술

- 🌀 **멸   치** : 멸치 2컵, 참기름 1큰술, 식용유 2큰술, 볶은깨 1큰술, 소스 3큰술

- 🌀 **감자 조림** : 감자(중간크기) 2½개를 사각으로 썰어 냄비에 물(1 ½ 컵) 붓고 익힌 뒤 감자 삶은 국물은 버리고 익은 감자만 – 소스 2큰술, 참기름 1큰술, 볶은깨 1큰술

- 🌀 **4 색 꼬치** : 새우, 홍합, 골뱅이, 스칼롭을 꼬치에 끼워 소스가 끓을 때 잠깐씩 적셔낸다.

- 🌀 **그   외** : 생선, 꼬타리, 북어, 콩조림, 작은 물오징어, 어묵 등 같은 방법으로 조리하면서 볶은고추장만 조금 넣으면 또 다른 맛을 낼 수 있다.

* 만들어놓은 소스는 냉동에 보관, 6개월 이상 두어도 변하지 않음.

🍲 For Basic Sauce

2 cups soy sauce, 10 cloves garlic, 2 tbsp. rice wine or wine, ½cup fish sauce*, ⅓ cup corn syrup, 6 tbsp. brown sugar, 3 cups ginger water (35 slices ginger plus 5 cups water, hot broil)

🍲 Making

In a saucepan, combine all the sauce ingredients and cook on high heat for 35~50 minutes. For everyday convenience, always have some on hand in the refrigerator. Basic Sauce can be used with many side dishes (see recipes) and kept frozen for six months.

*Note : Heat Basic Sauce in a skillet and, when boiling, add the ingredients of a side dish and stir-fry for 1-2 minutes.

* Available in Asian groceries.

Heat Basic Sauce (see separate recipe) in a skillet and, when boiling, add the ingredients of a side dish and stir-fry for 1-2 minutes.

- 🌀 **Dried Radish Side Dish** : 2½ cups dried radish*, softened in water 5 hours, rinsed and water squeezed out, 1 tbsp. sesame oil, ½ tbsp. seasoned hot chili paste*, 1 tsp. hot chili powder*, 1 tbsp. toasted sesame seeds*, 1 tbsp. sugar, ½ tbsp. Basic Sauce

- 🌀 **Seaweed and Fem Tips Side Dish** : 10 sheets toasted seaweed*, crumbled, 1 tbsp. sesame oil, 1 tbsp. toasted sesame seeds, 2½ tbsp. Basic Sauce, 1½ cups fern shoots*, squeezed, coarsely chopped

- 🌀 **Squid Side Dish** : 4 oz. dried, shredded squid*, 1 tbsp. toasted sesame seeds, 1 tbsp. sesame oil, 2½ tbsp. Basic Sauce

- 🌀 **Dried Anchovy Side Dish** : 2 cups dried anchovies*, 1 tbsp. sesame oil, 2 tbsp. cooking oil, 1 tbsp. toasted sesame seeds

- 🌀 **Potatoes Chorim Side Dish** : 3 small potatoes, in ½″ cubes, 1½ cups water, 1 tbsp. toasted sesame seeds, 1 tbsp. sesame oil, 2 tbsp. Basic Sauce

- 🌀 **Seafood Brochette Side Dish** : cooked shrimp, mussels, snails and fresh scallops skewers (bamboo or metal) or picks Basic Sauce

Add a shrimp, mussel, snail and fresh scallop to each skewer. Dip each skewer in the boiling Basic Sauce for half a minute or so to coat the seafood and cook the scallop.

Note : Fish, dried tiny fish, dried pollock*, softened black beans, tiny squid, fried bean curd, etc., can become their own side dishes when combined with some Basic Sauce and cooked 1-2 minutes.

* Available in Asian groceries.

1   2   3   4   5

(김) · 치 · 마 · 른 · 반 · 찬 · 류 (Kimchi and side dishes)

더덕구이(Spicy Codoropsis Root)

🍲 준비는 이렇게(4인분)

더덕 1 lb., 볶음 고추장 3큰술, Cooking wine 1큰술, 곱게 다진 마늘 1작은술, 진간장 1큰술, 흑설탕 3큰술, 참기름 2큰술

🍲 만드는 것은 이렇게

❶ 더덕은 골고루 잘 펴서 적당히 칼 뒷등으로 두들긴다.
❷ 재료를 잘 섞은 후 골고루 더덕에 발라 프라이팬에 참기름 1큰술을 붓고 타지 않도록 자주 뒤집어 주면서 구워낸다.
❸ 먹기 좋은 크기로 썰어 잣가루를 위에 고명으로 쓴다.

🍲 4 servings

1 lb. frozen codoropsis root*, thawed, 3 tbsp. hot chili paste*, 1 tbsp. cooking wine, 1 tsp. minced garlic, 1 tbsp. soy sauce, 3 tbsp. brown sugar, 3 tbsp. sesame oil, crushed pine nuts for garnish

🍲 Making

On a cutting board, pound the codoropsis root with the back edge of a knife and flatten to ¼″ thick. Combine the remaining ingredients, except 1 tablespoon of the sesame oil, and brush over the flattened root. In a non-stick skillet over medium-low heat, add 1 tablespoon sesame oil and slowly cook both sides of the codoropsis root. To serve, cut in bite sizes. Garnish with crushed pine nuts.

∗ Available in Asian groceries.

그린빈요리(Seasoned Green Beans) – 껍질콩

😊 준비는 이렇게(4인분)

그린빈 ¾ lb., 식용유 1½컵

😊 만드는 것은 이렇게

❶ 파란 긴콩(껍질콩)을 물에 씻지 말고 깨끗한 타월로 잘 닦아둔 다. 식용유 1½컵을 프라이팬에 붓고 기름이 달아오를 때 파란 긴 콩을 빨리 튀겨낸다.

❷ 섞어놓은 양념장을 프라이팬에 붓고 보글보글 끓을 때 튀겨놓 은 껍질콩을 넣고 뒤적거리면서 볶는 동안 양념이 골고루 묻도 록 한다. (센불에 2분 정도)

😊 양념 준비는 이렇게

참기름 1큰술, 후추 ¼작은술, 진간장 1½큰술, 볶은깨 1작은술, 고춧 가루 1작은술, 설탕 1큰술, 볶은고추장 1작은술, 정종 1작은술(양념재 료들을 혼합해 둠)

＊ 너무 오랫동안 튀기면 색깔이 곱지 않고, 또한너무 오래 볶으면 질겨진다.

😊 4 servings

¾ lb. green beans, cleaned by wiping with wet paper towels, 1½ cups cooking oil

😊 Making

Heat the cooking oil in a skillet, fry the green beans very quickly until they turn bright green and promptly remove with a slotted spoon. Combine the seasoning ingredients and heat the mixture in another skillet. When boiling, add the green beans and stir-fry over high heat for 2 minutes, evenly distributing the seasoning.

😊 For seasoning

1 tbsp. sesame oil, ¼ tsp. black pepper, 1 ½ tbsp. soy sauce, 1 tbsp. sugar, 1 tsp. rice wine, 1 tsp. toasted sesame seeds, 1 tsp. hot chili paste*, 1 tsp. hot chili powder*

＊Note : Green beans lose their crispy, fresh color if over fried and over cooking in the seasoning will toughen them.

＊Available in Asian groceries.

우엉조림(Burdock Root Cho-rim)

🍲 준비는 이렇게(4인분)

우엉(보통크기) 3개, 진간장 ⅓컵, 흑설탕 ⅓ 컵, 참기름 ⅓ 컵, 정종 2 큰술, 볶은깨 1큰술, 다진 마늘 1작은술, 베이킹소다 ¼작은술, 물 2컵

🍲 만드는 것은 이렇게

1. 먼저 우엉 껍질을 벗긴다.
2. 손가락 마디길이로 토막을 낸 뒤 먹기 좋은 크기로 채썬다.
3. 물 2컵을 붓고 베이킹 소다 ¼작은술을 넣고 15분 정도 팔팔 끓이면 먹기 좋게 연하게 된다.
4. 국물을 버리고 진간장과 흑설탕, 참기름, 다진 마늘, 정종, 볶은 통깨 등을 넣고 자작자작 국물이 없어질 때까지 조린다.

❋ 상에 낼 때 실고추와 잣을 고명한다.

🍲 4 servings

3 pieces burdock roots*, peeled, cut 1½ ″ strips, ¼ tsp. baking soda, 2 cups water, ⅓ cup dark soy sauce, ⅓ cup brown sugar, ⅓ cup sesame oil, 2 tbsp. sake (rice wine), 1 tbsp. toasted sesame seeds*, 1 tsp. garlic, minced, garnish with shredded red chili and pine nuts

🍲 Making

Place burdock roots and baking soda in a saucepan, add enough water (about 2 cups) to cover and boil for 15 minutes on medium high heat or until tender. Discard the water, add the remaining ingredients and continue cooking on medium low heat until sauce is reduced to a thick, slurpy consistency. Store in a tight container. To serve, garnish with shredded red chili and pine nuts.

❋ Available in Asian groceries.

김 · 치 · 마 · 른 · 반 · 찬 · 류 (Kimchi and side dishes)

콩조림(Black Beans in Soy Sauce)

준비는 이렇게

까만콩 600g, 물 9컵, 볶은깨 3큰술

소스 준비는 이렇게

진간장 1컵, 참기름 ⅓컵, 설탕 5큰술, 정종 1큰술, 후추 ½작은술, 납작 썬 생강 8쪽, 납작 썬 마늘 18쪽, 베이킹소다 1작은술

콩 삶기

❶ 까만콩은 판판한 그릇에 담고 잡티를 골라내고 물 9컵을 붓고 3시간 이상 불린 다음(불린 물은 버린다) 냄비에 다시 다른 물을 9컵 붓고 콩이 익을 때까지 끓인다.
❷ 베이킹소다 1작은술을 같이 넣고 삶으면 빨리 삶아진다.
❸ 35분 정도 센불에 삶고 나면 물도 많이 줄어들고 콩이 연해진다.
❹ 삶은 국물은 다 버리고 콩과 분리한다.

소스 만들기

소스 재료들을 모두 한데 넣고 3분쯤 보글보글 끓이다가 생강쪽과 마늘쪽은 향기만 빼고 버린다.

콩조림

❶ 위의 소스를 납작한 냄비에 분량대로 다 넣고 먼저 보글보글 끓을 때 삶아건져 놓은 콩을 소스에 넣고 자주 젓는다.
❷ 15분 정도 지나 되어 물기가 없어지면 볶은깨를 뿌리고 상에 낸다.

serving

600g black beans, 9 cups water, for soaking beans, 9 cups water, for cooking beans, 1 tsp. baking soda (optional), 3 tbsp. toasted sesame seeds for garnish

Making

Spread the black beans on a tray and remove any bad ones, then soak the good beans in water for 3 hours or more. Discard the water. In a saucepan, cook the beans in water until tender, about 35 minutes, on high heat (adding baking soda can speed up the cooking time). Drain and discard the water.

In a wide flat saucepan, combine all the sauce ingredients and boil for 3 minutes. Discard the ginger and garlic. Add the beans to the sauce and cook another 15 minutes, stirring frequently until liquid is reduced almost to none. Garnish with toasted sesame seeds before serving.

For sauce

1 cups soy sauce, ⅓cup sesame oil, 5 tbsp. sugar, 1 tbsp. sake (rice wine), 1 tsp. baking soda, 18 slices garlic, ½ tsp. black pepper, 8 slices ginger

(김) · 치 · 마 · 른 · 반 · 찬 · 류 (Kimchi and side dishes)

풋고추장아찌(Pickled Green Chilies)

🍳 준비는 이렇게

풋고추(맵지 않은 것) 2 lbs., 간장 2 컵, 설탕 ½ 컵, 물 1 컵, 소금 ⅓ 컵, 식초, 파 2뿌리(다진것), 미나리 ½단, 실백(잣) 1큰술

🍳 만드는 것은 이렇게

❶ 고추를 씻어 물기를 없앤 다음, 병에 담아 고추가 잠길 정도로 식초를 넣고 3~4일 후에 식초를 따라버린다.

❷ 간장, 소금, 물, 설탕을 넣고 1주 지난 후에 간장을 냄비에 넣고 끓인 후 식혀서 병에 담고 1주일 후에 다시 한번 끓여서 붓는다.

❸ 먹을 때 파, 깨소금, 참기름을 간하여 먹는다.

＊ 실백도 곱게 다져서 위에 뿌린다.

＊ 양념하지 않고 그냥 풋고추 장아찌만 먹어도 된다.

🍳 serving

2 lbs. mild green chilies (finger length), rinsed, patted dry, 2 cups soy sauce, ½ cup sugar, ⅓ cup salt, 1 cup water, vinegar as needed to cover, pine nuts for garnish, chopped spring onions (optional), toasted sesame seeds (optional), sesame oil (optional)

🍳 Making

Place chilies in a large bottle and gently press them down. Add enough vinegar to cover and let stand for 3-4 days. Discard the vinegar. Add a mixture of soy sauce, sugar, water and salt and let stand for a week. Pour the liquids out of the bottle into a sauce pan and boil for a few minutes. Cool and then pour the liquid back in the bottle over the chilies and store in a cool place or refrigerate.

This can either be served as is or mixed with chopped spring onions, toasted sesame seeds and sesame oil. Garnish with a few pine nuts.

무말랭이 오징어김치
(Dried Radish Kimchi with Dried squid)

준비는 이렇게

무말랭이 4oz(113g), 마른오징어 2마리(몸만), 찹쌀가루 ½컵, 물 2컵

만드는 것은 이렇게

❶ 무말랭이 4oz에 물 2리터를 붓고 밤새도록 12시간 이상 불린다.
❷ 마른오징어(중간크기) 2마리는 불에 구워 가위로 채썰어둔다.
❸ 찹쌀가루 ½컵에 물 2컵을 붓고 풀을 쑤어 식힌다.
❹ 양념장 재료들과 식힌 찹쌀풀을 잘 섞어 혼합한 후 불린 무말랭이와 구워 채썬 오징어를 같이 넣고 잘 버무린다.

양념 준비는 이렇게

고춧가루 ½컵, 물로 된 오징어젓갈 ¾컵(타일랜드 제품), 설탕 ⅓컵, 볶은깨 ½컵, 다진마늘 2큰술, 다진생강 1작은술, 정종 2큰술

＊ 3일 뒤부터 먹는다. 한국에서는 겨울철에 김장김치와 같이 만들어서 오래 두고 먹는다.
＊ 오징어젓갈 대신 멸치액젓을 써도 무방함.
＊ 오징어젓갈(타일랜드제품)은 동양식품에서 구입

serving

4 oz. dried radish*, 2 dried squid without tentacles, ½ cup glutinous rice flour*, water for soaking and cooking

Making

Soak the radish in 2 liters of water for 12 hours or longer. Rinse and drain. Grill the dried squid and cut into bite size pieces with kitchen shears. In a saucepan, heat the rice flour and 2 cups of water until thickening occurs, let cool.
For the seasoning, combine and gently mix the seven ingredients listed. Add the seasoning mixture to the thickened rice flour; then stir in the radish and squid. In three days the dish will be ready to eat.

For seasoning

½ cup hot chili paste*, ¾ cup liquid from brined squid*, ⅓ cup sugar, ½ cup toasted sesame seeds, 2 tbsp. minced garlic, 1 tsp. grated ginger, 2 tbsp. rice wine

＊Notes : In cold winter months, this dish can be preserved for a longer time. Brined anchovy liquid can substitute for brined squid liquid (from Thailand).
＊Available in Asian groceries.

김 · 치 · 마 · 른 · 반 · 찬 · 류 (Kimchi and side dishes)

굴깍두기(Radish Kimchi with Oysters)

🥚 준비는 이렇게(4인분)

무 2개(1kg), 굴 8oz(227g), 파 30g, 미나리 30g, 다진 마늘 3큰술, 다진 생강 1작은술, 고춧가루 ½컵. 새우젓 ¼컵, 설탕 2큰술, 소금 1큰술, 볶은깨 2큰술, 실고추 1작은술, 잣 1큰술, 소금 1작은술

🥚 만드는 것은 이렇게

❶ 무는 깨끗이 씻어서 먹기 좋은 크기로 깍둑썰기하여 소금 1큰술과 설탕 1큰술로 살짝 절여놓는다.

❷ 굴은 물에 살살 흔들어 씻어 건져놓고 물기를 빼놓는다..

❸ 미나리도 잎을 떼고 깨끗이 씻어 3cm 길이로 썰어 놓는다.

❹ 실파도 깨끗이 다듬어 씻어 미나리와 같은 길이로 썰어 놓는다.

❺ 마늘, 생강은 곱게 다지고 새우젓도 다져 놓는다. 넓은 그릇에 절인 무를 담고 다진 마늘과 생강, 고춧가루, 새우젓, 설탕 1큰술을 넣어 무가 빨갛게 물이 들도록 골고루 버무린다.

❻ 버무린 무에 실파와 미나리를 넣어 버무린 후 굴을 넣고 싱거우면 소금 1작은술을 넣고 볶은깨와 실고추, 잣을 넣고 꼭꼭 눌러둔다.

🥚 4 servings

2 radishes (about 2 lbs.) peeled, diced ½″, 1 tsp. salt, 2 tbsp sugar, 3 tbsp. garlic, minced, 30g spring onions, cut 1½″ long, 1 tsp. ginger, minced, ½ cup hot chili powder*, ¼ cup brined tiny shrimp*, (1″ long), minced, 8 oz. fresh oysters, rinsed in slightly salty water, 2 tbsp. toasted sesame seeds*, 1 tsp. shredded red chili*, 1 tbsp. pine nuts

🥚 Making

Sprinkle salt and 1 tablespoon sugar over the radishes and let stand for 30 minutes or until wilted. Combine the garlic, ginger, brined shrimp, chili powder and 1 tablespoon sugar and mix this into the radishes until they turn red from the chili powder. Gently toss the spring onions, oysters, shredded chili and pine nuts together and put all the ingredients in a bottle. Adjust the salt if needed and store in the refrigerator.

＊Available in Asian groceries.

썬김치 (Sliced Cabbage Kimchi)

준비는 이렇게

배추 3 lbs., 물 2컵, 소금 ⅓컵

만드는 것은 이렇게

❶ 배추는 3인치 정도의 크기로 썰어 미지근한 물 2컵에 소금 ⅓컵을 섞어 썰어놓은 배추에 붓고 7시간 정도 숨을 죽인 후 찬물에 3~4번 헹군 뒤에 소쿠리에 담아 물기를 뺀다.

❷ 무는 채썰어 놓고 나머지 양념은 분량대로 판판한 그릇에 담아 섞은 뒤 채썬 무를 넣어 버무린다. 여기에 소금에 절여 물기를 뺀 배추를 넣고 잘 버무린 뒤 병에 담고 12시간 뒤에 냉장고에 넣었다가 이틀 후부터 먹는다.

양념 준비는 이렇게

무 8 oz., 다진마늘 1큰술, 고춧가루 ½컵, 새우젓 2큰술, 멸치액젓 1큰술, 볶은깨 1큰술

serving

3 lbs. Napa cabbage, cut in 3″ lengths, 2 cups water, lukewarm, ⅓ cup salt

Making

Dissolve the salt in lukewarm water and sprinkle over cabbage. Cover and let stand for 7 hours. Rinse the cabbage 3 times in cold water and let drain in a colander.

Combine the kimchi sauce ingredients and mix thoroughly into the cabbage. Put the seasoned cabbage in a bottle, cover and let stand at room temperature for 12 hours. Refrigerate for a couple of days or until it reaches the desired level of fermentation.

For kimchi sauce

8 oz. radish, shredded, 1 tbsp. garlic, minced, ½ cup hot chili powder*, 2 tbsp. concentrated liquid from brined shrimp*, 1 tbsp. concentrated liquid from brined anchovy*, 1 tbsp. toasted sesame seeds

＊Available in Asian grocery.

김·치·마·른·반·찬·류 (Kimchi and side dishes)

오이소박이 (Stuffed Cucumber Kimchi)

준비는 이렇게

피클오이 10개, 소금 1/3컵, 설탕 1큰술, 무우 120g, 새우젓 1큰술, 고춧가루 2큰술, 다진마늘 1큰술, 다진 생강 1작은술, 채썬당근 1/2컵, 오징어액젓(타일랜드제품) 2큰술, 잣 1큰술, 볶은깨 1큰술, 물 2½컵

만드는 것은 이렇게

❶ 오이를 솔로 문질러 모래가 없도록 잘 씻은 후 중간에 4센티 길이로 칼집을 넣고 양끝이 0.4센티 되게 남긴다.

❷ 물 2½컵에 설탕 1큰술, 소금 1/3컵을 넣고 잘 저어 소금물을 만들어 오이에 붓고 30분 정도 절여둔다.

❸ 잘 절여진 오이는 위, 아래를 잡고 칼집이 쉽게 벌어지면 적당히 절여진 상태이므로 그대로 건져서 물에 한번 더 씻은 뒤 물기를 뺀다.

❹ 무는 곱게 채썰고 분량의 고춧가루에 버무려 둔다.

❺ 새우젓은 다져 오징어액젓과 같이 무와 섞은 다음 다진마늘과 다진생강을 넣고 골고루 잘 섞은 뒤 볶은깨와 잣을 넣는다.

❻ 채썬 당근도 넣는다.

❼ 오이를 손으로 잡고 눌러 칼집 사이를 벌리고 버무려 놓은 소박이 양념을 볼록할 정도로 넣는다.

❽ 양념 넣은 오이를 힘을 주어 꼭 쥐어준다.

❾ 김칫병에 차곡차곡 담고 양념묻은 그릇에 물을 약간 부어(싱거우면 소금마늘가루(갈릭솔트)를 약간 넣고 간을 맞춤) 소박이 위에 살짝 붓는다.

＊ 하룻밤을 밖에 두었다가 냉장고에 넣는다.

＊ 여름철에는 부추를 무와 같이 쓰면 별미가 된다.

＊ 소금에 절인 상태가 적당해야 오이가 아삭아삭하다.

serving

10 pickling size cucumbers, each 3-4″ long, 2½ cups water, 1 tbsp. sugar, 1/3 cup salt, ½ cup thin radish strips, ½ cup thin carrot strips

Making

Make a cut through the center section of each cucumber without cutting through the ends, then rotate a quarter turn, and make another cut, again, only through the center section. Marinate the cucumbers in a mixture of water, sugar and salt for about 30 minutes. Test by gently pushing a cucumber's ends together. When a cucumber yields and bows without cracking or breaking, it is ready to stuff.

Mix the seasoning ingredients and combine most of it with the radish and carrots to make the stuffing. Gently press the ends of a cucumber between your thumb and forefinger to open and fill the cuts with stuffing until plump. Lay the stuffed cucumbers side by side in a glass container.

Pour any leftover seasoning mixture over the cucumbers, adding more water to completely submerge them and garlic salt to taste. Cover tightly and leave at room temperature for 1 day. Then store in the refrigerator.

For seasoning

2 tbsp. hot chili powder, 1 tbsp. minced garlic, 1 tsp. grated ginger, 2 tbsp. liquid from brined squid*, 1 tbsp. pine nuts, 1 tbsp. toasted sesame seeds, 1 tbsp. liquid from brined tiny shrimp*

＊Note : In the summer, garlic chives can be a delicious ingredient for the stuffing.

＊Available in Asian groceries.

동치미(Mild Radish Kimchi, Dongchimi)

준비는 이렇게

무(중간크기) 8개, 파 1단, 풋고추 10개, 마늘 2통, 생강 4쪽, 붉은 고추 2개, 배 1개, 소금 1½컵, 소금마늘가루 ½컵, 당근(중간크기) 2개, 찹쌀 가루 1큰술, 양파 1개, 설탕 2큰술, 물 22컵

만드는 것은 이렇게

❶ 중간 크기의 무는 반으로 잘라 깨끗이 씻어 소금 1½컵에 굴려 잰다.(하룻동안)

❷ 풋고추는 꼭지째 소금 1큰술+물 3컵에 이틀 정도 담갔다가 깨 끗이 꼭꼭 눌러 닦아놓는다. 파는 어슷어슷 크게 3등분 썰어놓 는다.

❸ 마늘은 얄팍하게 저며 썰어놓고 생강도 4쪽 썰어놓는다. 당근 도 채썰고 배는 껍질째 잘 씻어 4등분하고 씨는 뺀다. 붉은 고 추는 잘 씻어놓는다.

❹ 절인 무는 헹구어서 물기를 빼고 김칫병에 담고 ②와 ③을 모두 차곡차곡 넣는다.

❺ 물 2컵에 찹쌀가루를 풀고 양파를 ½로 잘라 넣어 팔팔 끓인 뒤 완전히 식으면 양파는 버리고 그 식은 물에 물 약 20컵을 소금 ½컵과 설탕 2큰술을 타서 섞어 ④에 붓는다.

＊ 이틀동안 밖에 두었다가 냉장고에 넣는다.
   마늘을 더 넣고 싶을 때는 다진 마늘을 헝겊에 싸서 띄운다.
   (국물이 깨끗해야 됨)

＊ 상에 낼 때 실파와 잣을 띄운다.

serving

10 green chilies with stem attached, 1½ cups salt, 8 medium radishes, cut in halves, 2 red chilies, 2 medium carrots, cut into thin strips, 5-6 spring onions, cut into thirds, 1 Asian pear, unpeeled, cored and cut in quarters, 2 bulbs garlic, sliced, 4 slices ginger, 1 tbsp. glutinous rice flour*, 22 cups water, 1 onion, cut in half, ½ cup garlic salt, 2 tbsp. sugar, pine nuts and shredded red chilies for garnish

Making

Soak the green chilies in water salted with ¼ cup of salt for 2 days, then gently squeeze out the water and pat the chilies dry. Sprinkle the radish pieces with 1¼ cup of salt and let stand overnight. Rinse thoroughly.

In a large bottle, put the radishes, green chilies, red chilies, carrots, spring onions, pear, garlic and ginger slices. In a saucepan, add the onion to 2 cups of water and bring to a boil. Let cool, discard the onion and add 20 cups of water, the garlic salt and sugar. Pour this into the bottle with the vegetables, let stand for 2 days at room temperature, then refrigerate. If more garlic is needed, wrap minced garlic in cheesecloth, tie tightly and let it float in the bottle. This will keep the kimchi juice clear.

When serving, garnish with pine nuts and shredded red chilies.

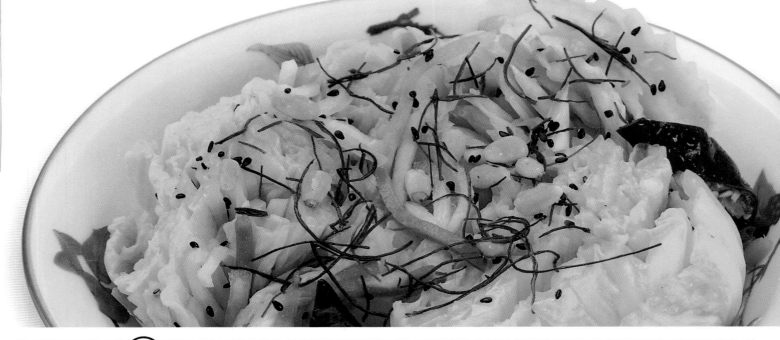

김 · 치 · 마 · 른 · 반 · 찬 · 류 (Kimchi and side dishes)

백김치(Mild Cabbage Kimchi)

🥢 준비는 이렇게

배추 5포기, 무(중간크기) 2개, 밤 10개, 배 3개, 마늘 2통, 생강 2쪽, 파 4뿌리, 당근 2개, 양파 2개, 소금 4컵, 소금마늘가루 ⅓컵, 실고추 약간, 잣 3큰술, 찹쌀가루 1큰술, 물 20컵

🥢 만드는 것은 이렇게

❶ 배추는 길이로 길게 4등분하여 배추가 물에 잠길 정도로 소금 4컵을 붓고 푹 절인다.(하룻동안)

❷ 절인 배추를 깨끗이 씻어 물기를 뺀다.

❸ 무, 밤, 배, 마늘, 생강, 당근, 파는 채썰어 놓는다.

❹ 양파 2개를 4등분으로 크게 자르고 찹쌀가루 1큰술과 물 3컵에 넣어 팔팔 끓여 식혀놓는다. 식으면 양파는 버리고 국물만 쓴다.

❺ ❸번과 잣, 실고추를 넣고 소금마늘가루 ⅓컵을 넣어 같이 버무린다.

❻ 절여진 배추의 갈피갈피에 버무린 소(❺)를 채워넣고 김칫병에 차곡차곡 눌러 담는다.

❼ ❹의 찹쌀 끓여 식힌 물에 물 20컵을 붓고 싱거우면 소금을 조금씩 조심성있게 넣고 ❻의 배추 위에 자작자작할 정도로 채운다.

✳ 국물이 너무 많아도 싱겁고 적으면 더욱 좋지 않다. 배추에 자작할 정도로 충분히 채운다.

✳ 기호에 따라 표고버섯을 불려 채썰어 넣기도 하고 대춧물을 우려 넣기도 한다.

✳ 대춧물 우리기 : 통대추 10개 정도에 물 3컵을 붓고 끓인다.
   5~7분 후에 빨간 대추색이 우러나면 대추는 버리고 국물만 쓴다.

🥢 serving

5 Napa cabbages, cut lengthwise in quarters, 4 cups salt, 2 medium radishes, cut into strips, 10 chestnuts, cut into strips, 3 pears, cut in strips, 2 ginger roots, cut in strips, 2 carrots, cut in strips, 2 bulbs garlic, cut into strips, 4 springs onions, cut into strips, 2 tbsp. pine nuts, ⅓ cup garlic salt, 1 tsp. shredded red chili, 2 onions, quartered, 1 tbsp. glutinous rice flour, water as needed, salt as needed

🥢 Making

Combine salt and enough water to submerge the cabbage and let stand over night until completely wilted. Rinse thoroughly and drain. Combine the cabbage, the radishes, chestnuts, pears, ginger, carrots, garlic and spring onion. Add the pine nuts, shredded red chili and garlic salt. Stuff this mixture between each of the wilted cabbage leaves, fold in half and pack tightly into a large bottle.

In saucepan, combine 3 cups water, glutinous rice powder and onions and bring to a boil. Let cool and discard the onion pieces. Add 20 cups of water and slowly pour into the bottle over the cabbage until barely covered.

✳ Note : Liquid from red dates as well as black mushrooms can also be added to suit taste preferences. To prepare red date liquid, boil 10 reddates in 3 cups water for 5-7 minutes, and discard the dates.

보쌈김치 (Cabbage Leaf Wrapped Kimchi)

준비는 이렇게

배추 2포기, 무(중간크기) ½개, 배 ½개, 밤 4개, 대추 3개, 불린표고버섯 2개, 파 2뿌리, 마늘다진 것 2큰술, 당근 1개, 채썬 생강 1큰술, 굴 80g, 낙지 2마리, 동태 1마리(3인치정도 3쪽), 새우젓 ⅓컵, 고춧가루 ⅔컵, 잣 1큰술, 까만깨 1큰술, 실고추 약간, 소금 2컵, 설탕 2큰술

만드는 것은 이렇게

❶ 배추는 포기를 갈라서 소금물에 절였다가 씻어 물기를 뺄 때 설탕 2큰술을 골고루 뿌려둔다. 보자기로 쌀 겉잎은 충분히 떼어놓고 속잎만 모아 3~4센티 길이로 썬다.

❷ 무와 배는 껍질 벗겨 배추크기로 썰고 껍질 벗긴 밤도 얇게 썰어놓는다.

❸ 마늘과 생강은 곱게 다진다. 파는 3센티 길이로 썬다. 대추는 씨를 빼고 채썰고 불린 표고버섯과 당근도 채썬다. 낙지는 깨끗이 씻어 잘게 썰고 굴도 껍질을 가려내고 물기를 완전히 뺀 뒤 소금을 약간(¼작은술) 뿌려준다.

❹ 동태는 뼈를 바르고 잘게 썰어둔다. 소금을 약간 뿌린다. (¼작은술)

❺ 새우젓도 잘게 다진다.

❻ ①의 배추 썰어놓은 것과 ② ~ ⑤를 한데 섞고 고춧가루와 까만깨를 넣어 잘 섞는다.

❼ 절인 배추 겉잎을 보시기에 깔고 재료 ⑥을 정돈해서 잘 넣은 다음 위에다 실고추, 잣을 고명으로 얹어 잘 싸서(속이 보이지 않아야 됨) 병이나 항아리에 차곡차곡 담는다.

＊ 보쌈김치는 1인분씩 작게 만들어 꺼내먹기 좋게, 상에 낼때는 젓가락 으로 윗부분을 살짝 펼쳐 속이 잘 보이도록 한다.

＊ 일주일쯤 있다가 먹으면 좋고 해물과 젓국이 많이 들었으므로 빨리 익을 수 있으니 일찍 먹을수록 좋다.

serving

2 Napa cabbages, each cut lengthwise in half, 2 cups salt, dissolved in 6 cups of water, 2 tbsp. sugar, ½ medium radish, peeled and cut in 1½″ thin square slices, ½ Asian pear*, peeled, cored and cut similar to the radish, 4 chestnuts, shelled, blanched, cut in thin slices, 2 black mushrooms, softened in water, cut into strips, 2 spring onions, cut in 1″ pieces, 1 medium carrot, cut in thin strips, 2 tbsp. minced garlic, 1 tbsp. grated ginger, 3 pitted red dates*, cut in strips, 2 fresh squid, peeled, cleaned, cut in thin strips, ½ tsp. salt, 3 pollack (3″ long), fresh or frozen, deboned, diced ½″, sprinkled with ¼ tsp. salt, 80g oysters, rinsed, drained and sprinkled with ¼ tsp. salt, ½ cup brined tiny shrimp*, finely chopped, ⅔ cup hot chili powder, 1 tbsp. black sesame seeds*, 1 tbsp. pine nuts shredded red chili for garnish

Making

Submerge the cabbage in the salt water overnight or until totally wilted. Thoroughly rinse the wilted cabbage and drain. Reserve the leaf tops as wrappers. Cut the inner parts of the cabbage and the stalks of the outer leaves into 1-1½″ slices and sprinkle with sugar.
In a large mixing bowl, combine all the ingredients except the chili powder, black sesame seeds, pine nuts and shredded red chili, and then add the chili powder and black sesame seeds and mix well. Line a small shallow bowl with a single layer of the leaf tops, allowing them to drape over the rim. Spoon a portion of this mixture onto the leaves in the bowl, garnish with pine nuts and shredded red chili, and fold the draped leaves over the mixture. Carefully lift the wrap out of the bowl, making sure the leaves remain firmly in place, and fit the wrap snugly in a jar. Repeat the process with the remaining mixture and leaves. Store at room temperature. The kimchi will be ready to serve within a week. When serving, partially unwrap the top outer leaves like a flower bud unfolding. Keep refrigerated thereafter.

＊Note : The size of the kimchi will vary according to the amount of filling used.

＊Available in Asian groceries.

(김) · 치 · 마 · 른 · 반 · 찬 · 류 (Kimchi and side dishes)

나박김치(Light Kimchi, Nah-baak Kimchi)

🍲 준비는 이렇게

(큰 김칫병 기준), 배추(줄기) ½포기, 무(작은 것) 1개, 고추 1큰술, 마늘 3쪽, 생강즙 ½작은술, 파 2뿌리, 미나리 조금, 소금 1½큰술, 설탕 1큰술, 실백, 실고추

🍲 만드는 것은 이렇게

❶ 마늘, 생강, 고추의 즙을 내어 물기만 빼쓴다. 마른 고추일 때는 끓는 물에 넣어 즙을 낸다.

❷ 배추는 3센티 길이로 썰어 소금에 절이고 무는 2.5센티 길이로 얄팍하게 썰어 소금, 설탕과 마늘, 생강, 고추즙에 절인다.

❸ 배추 절인 것과 무를 병에 담아 미지근한 물을 싱겁게 간을 하여 병에 담고 같은 온도(물 온도)에 익힌다.

❹ 냉장고에 넣을 때 파 채썬 것과 미나리를 넣는다.

❺ 상에 놓을 때 실고추, 실백을 띄워 놓는다.

🍲 serving

½ head Napa cabbage, cut in 1″ slices, 1 small radish (½ lb.), cut in 1″ cubes, then sliced ⅛″ thick, 1½ tbsp. salt, 1 tbsp. chili powder* or minced fresh or red chili, 3 cloves garlic, minced, 3 slices ginger, minced or ½ tsp. ginger juice, 1 tbsp. sugar, 2 spring onions, cut into strips, water as needed, shredded chili and pine nuts for garnish

🍲 Making

Sprinkle 1 tablespoon of salt over the cabbage and let wilt. Mix the garlic, ginger, chili powder and 2 tablespoons of water, then strain to extract the juice. Add this juice, ½ tablespoon salt and the sugar to the radish cubes and let wilt.

Pour the cabbage and radishes in a bottle and fill with lightly salted lukewarm water. Adjust seasoning with salt to taste. Store at room temperature until fermented (some bubbles will appear). Add the spring onions and refrigerate. This dish will keep in the refrigerator for as long as 2 weeks.

When serving, garnish with shredded red chilies and pine nuts.

* Available in Asian groceries.

밥 · 류 (Rice dishes)

카레라이스(Rice with Curry Sauce)

😊 준비는 이렇게(5인분)

S.B.카레(8.4oz,240g), 쇠고기 ½lb., 감자(중간크기) 5개, 양파(중간크기) 3개, 당근(중간크기) 2개, 후추 ½작은술, 물 5컵, 3컵 씻은쌀, 3½컵 밥물

😊 만드는 것은 이렇게

❶ 기름기 없는 쇠고기는 잘 씻어 깍둑썰기로 썰어 놓는다.

❷ 감자는 껍질을 벗기고 씻은 다음 깍둑 썰고 양파도 껍질을 벗겨 씻은 후 깍둑 썬다.

❸ 당근도 껍질을 벗기고 씻어 깍둑썰기한다.

❹ 판판하고 오목한 중간냄비에 썰어놓은 쇠고기를 넣고 볶는다.

❺ 고기가 다 익을 때까지(3분정도)감자와 양파,당근을 넣고 물 5컵을 넣고 후추 ½작은술 넣고 끓인다.

❻ 끓고부터 3분 지난 뒤 S.B 카레를 냄비에 넣고 잘 젓는다.

❼ 센불에서 약간 낮은불로 카레가 다 풀어지고 걸쭉해질 때까지 끓인다. (3~4분 정도)

😊 밥 짓는 법

쌀 3컵을 3~4번 정도 물에 씻은 뒤 물 3½컵을 넣고 전기밥솥에 30~35분쯤 두면 밥이 된다.

* 판판한 접시에 다 된 밥을 담고 밥 위에 카레를 얹는다.

* 쇠고기 대신 닭고기를 써도 된다. 닭고기 양도 쇠고기와 같이 하고 물 5컵 대신 기름기없는 닭국물 5컵을 써야 제맛이 난다.

* 카레는 Golden Curry – Sauce Mix된 것을 쓰면 좋다. (동양식품이나 서양식품에서 구입)

😊 5 servings

1 pkg. S.B. curry sauce mix (8.4 oz.)*, ½ lb. lean beef, cut into ½″ cubes, 5 medium potatoes, diced in ½″ cubes, 3 medium size onions, diced in ½″ sizes, 2 carrots, diced in ½″ sizes, ½ tsp. black pepper, 3 cups rice, well washed, 8½ cups water

😊 Making

In a saucepan, brown the beef, about 3 minutes, and add the onions, carrots, potatoes, black pepper and 5 cups of water. Bring to a boil and cook for 3 minutes. Add the curry sauce mix, stirring continuously until thick. Lower the heat and cook for another 3 or 4 minutes. Cook 3 cups rice in an electric rice cooker with 3½cups water for 30-35 minutes or until the "done" light illuminates. Serve the beef curry over the rice.

* Notes : Chicken can substitute for beef, and chicken stock may be used instead of water.
  The brand name of S.B. curry is Golden Curry, which comes in solid squares.

* Available in Asian groceries.

비빔밥(Rice with Vegetables, Bi-bim Pahp)

🍲 준비는 이렇게(5인분)

쇠고기 ⅓ lb., 무 1.4 lb.(중간크기 1개), 콩나물 1 lb., 당면 3.4 oz, 오이(피클용) 3개, 시금치 0.6 lb., 물고비 4 oz., 캬베츠 0.4 lb., 달걀 2개

🍲 만드는 것은 이렇게

❶ 쇠고기는 채썰어 진간장 2큰술, 물½컵 넣고 볶아둔다. 무 1.4 lb.(중간크기 1개)를 반으로 나누어 놓는다.

❷ 반으로 나눈 무를 곱게 채썰어 고춧가루 1작은술 넣고 빨갛게 물들인다.

❸ 물들인 무에 다시 고춧가루 ½큰술, 참기름 ½작은술, 다진마늘 ½작은술, 소금마늘가루(갈릭솔트) ½작은술, 볶은깨 1큰술, 식초 ½작은술을 넣고 무친다.

❹ 나머지 반으로 나눈 무는 물⅓컵, 소금마늘가루(갈릭솔트) ½작은술, 참기름 ½작은술, 다진마늘 ½작은술을 넣고 냄비에 볶아놓는다.

❺ 콩나물(1 lb.)은 깨끗이 씻어 물 2컵을 붓고 삶아놓는다. 당면(3.4oz.)은 팔팔 끓는물 2컵에 삶아 찬물에 헹군 뒤 먹기 좋은 크기(4인치 정도)로 잘라 물기를 빼고 삶아놓은 콩나물과 같이 진간장 1½큰술, 참기름 1½큰술, 볶은깨 1큰술을 넣고 조물조물 무친다.

❻ 깨끗이 씻은 피클용 오이는 반달 모양으로 얇게 썰어 식초 1작은술, 소금마늘가루(갈릭솔트)½작은술, 참기름 1큰술, 볶은깨 1큰술 넣고 무친다.

❼ 시금치 0.6lb.는 깨끗이 씻어 물 2컵이 팔팔 끓을 때 1분 정도 삶는다. 찬물에 흙이 없도록 잘 씻어 물기를 꼭 짜고 참기름1큰술, 소금 마늘가루 ½작은술, 볶은통깨 1큰술 넣고 무쳐놓는다.

❽ 물고비도 깨끗이 씻은 후에 프라이팬에 참기름 1큰술, 진간장 1큰술, 볶은깨 1큰술 넣고 볶아놓는다.

❾ 캬베츠 0.4 lb.(중간크기 ¼쪽)는 껍질을 벗기고 곱게 채썰어 식초 ½작은술, 고춧가루 1큰술, 참기름 1큰술, 볶은깨 1큰술, 설탕 1큰술, 소금마늘가루 ½작은술을 넣고 무친다.

❿ 준비가 다 되면 넓은 대접에 밥을 2주걱 담고 각종 나물을 색깔 맞추어 색색이 놓고 중앙 한복판에 볶은 쇠고기를 놓은 다음 달걀 지단이나 달걀 반숙을 얹는다.

🍲 양념은 이렇게(분량은 만드는 법에 표시)

참기름, 볶은깨, 고춧가루, 소금마늘가루, 진간장, 식초, 고추장 7up

＊비빔밥 고추장 만들기 : 볶은고추장 2큰술, 참기름 1½큰술, 볶은깨 1큰술, 7up 2큰술 넣고 잘 버무려서 밥 비빌 때 적당히 1큰술 정도 넣고 비빔하면 된다.

＊밥 짓는 법 : 쌀 3컵, 물 3½컵 비율로 자동전기밥솥에서 30~35분 정도 되면 밥이 된다.

🍲 5 servings

⅓ lb. beef, cut in thin strips, 3 cups rice, 3½ tbsp. dark soy sauce, 1 medium radish (1.4 lb), cut in thin strips, 1½ tbsp. red chili powder, 7⅓ tbsp. sesame oil, 1 tsp. minced garlic, 2 tsp. garlic salt , 6-7 tbsp. toasted sesame seeds, 1 lb. soy bean sprouts*, 1½ tbsp. sesame oil, 3 tbsp. toasted sesame seeds, 3.4 oz. transparent noodles, 3 pickling cucumbers, 0.6 lb. spinach leaves, 4 oz. pre-soaked fern shoots, drained, 0.4 lb. cabbage (¼ medium one), 2 tbsp. prepared chili paste (Koh-chu-chang), 2 tbsp. Seven Up (beverage), fried egg strips for garnish

🍲 Making

In an electric rice cooker, cook the rice in 3½ cups of water for 30-40 minutes or until "done" light illuminates. Combine beef, 2 tablespoons soy sauce and ½ cup water and stir-fry until cooked. Divide the radish strips into 2 equal portions. Dye one portion red with 1 teaspoon red chili powder. Mix in another ½ tablespoon chili powder and ½ teaspoon each of sesame oil, minced garlic and garlic salt, and 1 tablespoon toasted sesame seed. Stir-fry the rest of the radish with ⅓ cup water and ½ teaspoon each of garlic salt, sesame oil and minced garlic.

Rinse bean sprouts, cook in 2 cups water and drain. Combine with 1½ tablespoons soy sauce, 1½ tablespoons sesame oil and 1 tablespoon toasted sesame seeds and gently mix. Cook the noodles in 2 cups of boiling water, rinse and drain. Cut into 4″ lengths and season the same as for bean sprouts above.

Cut cucumbers lengthwise, then cross-wise into thin semi-circular shapes. Mix and season with 1 teaspoon vinegar, ½teaspoon garlic salt, 1 tablespoon each of sesame oil and toasted sesame seeds. Blanch spinach leaves in 2 cups boiling water for a minute. Drain well and mix with 1 tablespoon sesame oil, ½ teaspoon garlic salt and 1 tablespoon toasted sesame seeds.

Wash fern shoots and season with 1 tbsp. each of sesame oil, soy sauce and toasted sesame seeds; then stir-fry. Peel off outer cabbage leaves and discard. Cut remaining cabbage into thin strips and season with 1½ tsp. of vinegar and 1 tbsp. of each of hot chili powder, sesame oil, sesame seeds, sugar and ½ tsp. of garlic salt.

For a seasoned hot chili paste, combine 2 tablespoons prepared chili paste (Koh-chu-chang), 1½ tablespoons sesame oil, 1 tablespoon toasted sesame seeds and 2 tablespoons 7-Up.

In individual bowls, place 2 serving spoonfuls of rice, center some beef on top and surround with vegetables, artfully arranged. Garnish each bowl with egg strips. When ready to eat, mix in seasoned hot chili paste according to individual taste.

＊Available in Asian groceries.

밥 · 류 (Rice dishes)

회덮밥(Rice Topped with Raw Fish)

준비는 이렇게(5인분)

참치(튜나) ½ lb., 도미 ½ lb., 갑오징어 ½ lb., 게살 ½ lb., 양상추(중간크기) 1개, 씨없는 오이 1개, 배 1개, 열무 무(빨간색 아주 작은 것)

만드는 것은 이렇게

❶ 양념장을 분량대로 합하여 잘 섞어 만들어 놓는다.
❷ 모든 생선과 해물은 먹기 좋은 굵은채(가로 0.5인치, 세로 2인치)로 썰어놓는다.
❸ 양상추도 채썰어놓고 오이와 빨간색 작은 무는 깨끗이 씻어 껍질째 반달로 썰고 배는 껍질 벗겨 굵직하게(가로 0.25인치, 세로 2인치) 채썰어 놓는다.
❹ 대접에 따뜻한 밥을 담고 밥 위에 야채와 생선을 모양있게 담고 먹기 전에 참기름을 1큰술 밥에 놓고 양념장은 먹어보면서 더 첨가한다.

양념장은 이렇게

강판에 갈아놓은 무 3큰술, 강판에 간 배 3큰술, 강판에 간 Turnips 2큰술, 양파 간 것 2큰술, 파 3뿌리(잘게다짐), 볶은깨 2큰술, 식초 3큰술, 볶은고추장 3½큰술, 잣 1큰술, 후추 ½작은술, 소금마늘가루 ½큰술, 설탕 2큰술, 정종 2큰술

＊ 생선 종류는 삶은 새우나 혹은 다른 어떤 것을 써도 된다.

5 servings

½ lb. fresh tuna, cut in bite sized (½" x 2") pieces, ½ lb. fresh snapper filet, cut in bite sized pieces, ½ lb. fresh squid, cut in strips, ½ lb. imitation crabsticks, cut in strips, 1 medium head of lettuce, shredded, 1 seedless cucumber, cut in strips, 5 salad sized red radishes, sliced, 1 Asian pear*, peeled, cored, cut in ¼" x 2" strips, 5 cups cooked rice, 1 tbsp. sesame oil

Making

Combine the ingredients for the seasoned soy sauce. In an individual serving bowl, place 1 cup of rice and colorfully arrange some of the other ingredients, except the sesame oil and seasoned soy sauce, on top. As the final touch, sprinkle each serving with sesame oil. Serve the seasoned soy sauce on the side to be added to individual taste.

For seasoned soy sauce

3 tbsp. grated radish, 3 tbsp. grated pear, 2 tbsp. grated turnip, 2 tbsp. grated onion, 3 tbsp. vinegar, 3 spring onions, finely chopped, 2 tbsp. toasted sesame seeds, 3½ tsp. hot chili paste*, 2 tbsp. sugar, 2 tbsp. rice wine, ½ tbsp. garlic salt, 1 tbsp. pine nuts, ½ tsp. black pepper

＊Note : Different seafood varieties and combinations may be also be substituted.
＊Available in Asian groceries.

볶음밥(Fried Rice, Bok—eum Pahp)

준비는 이렇게(4인분)

길쭉한 쌀 15.8oz.(448g)—(Uncle Bens/Boil-in-Bag Rice), 잔새우 0.38 lb., 송이버섯 0.35 lb., 쇠고기 0.32 lb., 물에 불린 표고버섯 3장, 파란 완두콩 ½컵(0.2lb.)(Frozen), 당근 (중간크기) 1개, 양파(중간크기) 1개, 파 3뿌리, 캬베츠 3잎, 식용유 ½컵+3큰술, 진간장 ⅓컵, 볶은깨(흰색, 까만색) 1½큰술, 달걀 3개, 게맛살(3인치) 6피스, 참기름 2큰술

만드는 것은 이렇게

❶ 판판한 냄비에 물을 넉넉히 붓고 물이 팔팔 끓으면 쌀(1box에 4봉지 들어 있음) 4봉지를 봉지째 넣고 10분간 끓인 뒤에 다 된 밥을 봉지에서 꺼내고 물은 버린다.

❷ 오목하고 판판한 프라이팬에 식용유 ½컵을 붓고 짜자자 소리가 나며 끓을 때 밥을 프라이팬에 붓고 볶는다.(2분 정도)

❸ 송이버섯, 당근, 양파, 표고버섯, 캬베츠는 잘게 깍둑 썰어놓고 쇠고기는 잘게 썰어놓고 새우는 삶아져 있으므로 잘 씻어놓는다.

❹ 파는 채썰고 게맛살도 잘게 썰어놓는다.

❺ 달걀은 프라이팬에 붓고 휘저어 덩어리가 부서지게 구워 놓는다.

❻ 냉동된 완두콩은 물에 씻어 얼음기를 빼고 채에 받쳐둔다.

❼ 다시 프라이팬에 식용유 3큰술을 넣고 쇠고기를 볶다가 익으면 당근을 넣고, 캬베츠, 양파, 표고, 송이 등을 넣어가며 볶는다. 거기에 새우와 게맛살을 넣고 그 다음에 완두콩, 만들어 놓은 달걀, 다진파를 순서대로 넣고 볶는다. 그리고 다 되면 미리 볶아 놓았던 밥에 진간장과 참기름을 넣어 1분 정도 볶고 볶은깨를 뿌린다.

＊ 볶음밥에 쇠고기 대신 닭고기를 넣어도 훌륭하고 햄, 돼지고기, 소세지 등을 넣어도 된다.

＊ 식성에 따라 간을 더하고 싶은 분은 소금을 써야 된다. 분량 이상의 간장을 넣으면 질어지고 볶음밥의 생명이 없어진다.

4 servings

1 box Uncle Bens long grain Boil-in-Bag rice (4 packages per box), ½ cup cooking oil, ⅓ lb. beef, coarsely chopped, 3 tbsp. cooking oil, 1 medium carrot, peeled, diced in ¼″ pieces, 1 medium onion, diced, ⅓ lb. fresh button mushrooms, diced to a similar size, 3 cabbage leaves, diced to a similar size, 6 imitation crabsticks, each 3″ long, diced to a similar size, ⅓ lb. tiny cooked salad shrimp, excess water removed, ½ cup frozen peas, 3 eggs, scrambled, 3 spring onions, chopped, ⅓ cup soy sauce, 1½ tbsp. toasted sesame seeds, 2 tbsp. sesame oil

Making

Cook all 4 packages of rice in boiling water according to the package instructions. In a heavy skillet, heat ½ cup of cooking oil and stir-fry rice until sizzling, about 2 minutes.

In another skillet, heat 3 tablespoons cooking oil, brown beef and stir-fry the carrot. Add the cabbage, onion and mushrooms, and then add the shrimp and crabsticks. Add the peas, eggs and spring onion while stirring continuously. Season with soy sauce, sesame oil and sesame seeds, and stir-fry one more minute.

＊Notes : Chicken, pork, ham or sausage may be substituted for the beef. To adjust saltiness, use salt rather than soy sauce, which can make rice soggy.

김밥소개(Sushi, Kim-pahp)

김밥은 그 속 재료에 따라서 여러 가지 모양과 맛으로 스타일이 변할 수 있다.

Using some basic ingredients, and depending on the method of preparation, one can create several varieties of sushi.
These basic ingredients will make 5 servings.

---

* 기본 재료 (5인분)

1. 밥 : 쌀 3 컵, 물 3 ½ 컵(보통 밥 짓듯이 함 – 30분 정도), 식초 2 ½큰술, 설탕 1 ½큰술, 소금 ⅛작은술을 밥과 혼합, 부채로 부치면서 3분 정도 식힌다.

2. 쇠고기 : ¾lb. (길이 3인치, 넓이 ½인치로 썬다.) 기꼬망간장 2 ½ 큰술, 브라운 설탕 2 큰술, 1큰술, 후추 ¼작은술을 고기와 혼합, 5분 정도 프라이팬에 조린다.

3. 달걀 : 3개
   소금 ¼작은술, 식물성 기름 1큰술 달걀과 소금을 잘 저어 섞어 기름에 프라이 하여 지단을 만들고 길이 6인치, 넓이 ½ 인치로 채썬다.

4. 게살 : 4 oz.
   잘게 찢어 소금 ⅛작은술을 넣고 분홍색 물감(food color)을 이쑤시개에 조금 묻혀 골고루 주물러 무쳐서 프라이팬에 2~3분 정도 볶는다.

5. 당근 : 보통크기 3개 (채로 썬다.)
   식초 1½큰술, 설탕 1큰술, 소금 ⅛작은 술을 채썬 당근과 같이 혼합, 골고루 주물러 꼭꼭 눌러 10분 정도 뒤에 다시 꼭 물기를 짠다.

6. 시금치 : 1lb. (팔팔 끓는 물 6컵에 데쳐 3~4번 찬물에 헹군 뒤 물기를 빼기 위해 꼭 짠다.) 참기름 1큰술, 소금 ½작은술, 통깨 1큰술을 시금치와 혼합, 주물러 무친다.

---

1. Rice : 3 cups rice, $3\frac{1}{2}$ cups water, $2\frac{1}{2}$ tbsp. vinegar, $1\frac{1}{2}$ tbsp. sugar, $\frac{1}{8}$ tsp. salt
Cook the rice with water according to rice cooker instructions.
When the rice is somewhat cool, gently sprinkle and combine it with the vinegar, salt and sugar mixture.

2. Beef : 3/4 lb. beef, cut in 3″ x ½″ strips, $2\frac{1}{2}$ tbsp. soy sauce, 2 tbsp., brown sugar, 1 tsp. sesame oil, ¼ tsp. black pepper
Combine and then gently mix the four other ingredients into the beef and cook for 5 minutes in a hot skillet or until beef sizzles.

3. Eggs : 3 eggs, ¼ tsp. salt, 1 tbsp. cooking oil
Lightly beat the eggs and salt with a fork and fry in a hot, oiled pan to make a pancake. Cut the pancake in 6″ x ½″ strips.

4. Imitation crabsticks (fish cakes)
4 oz.crabsticks, hand shredded, 1/8 tsp. salt, pink food coloring
Dip a toothpick in the food coloring and dab a little color on the crab, use a fork to distribute the color evenly, salt and stir-fry 2-3 minutes on low heat.

5. Carrots : 3 carrots, cut in thin strips, $1\frac{1}{2}$ tbsp. vinegar,1 tbsp.sugar 1/8 tsp. salt
Combine ingredients, let stand for 10 minutes and then gently squeeze out the juice.

6. Spinach : 1 lb. spinach leaves, 1 tbsp.sesame oil,1 tbsp. sesame seeds, 1 tsp. salt
Blanch the spinach in boiling water, quickly rinse in cold water, then gently squeeze out the liquid and combine the spinach with the other three ingredients.

밥 · 류 (Rice dishes)

막기김밥(Rolled Sushi)

😋 만드는 것은 이렇게

김 한 장을 깔고 김 반 장을 깐 김 위에 앞쪽으로 겹쳐 깐 다음 밥 1주걱 반 정도를 김 위에 놓고 손끝에 물을 약간씩 적셔가면서 밥을 끝까지 판판하게 편 다음 준비한 기본재료인 쇠고기, 달걀, 게맛살, 당근, 시금치를 밥 위에 가지런히 놓고 돌돌 만다.

😋 Making

nori sheets*
prepared rice (#1 from Basic Sushi)
prepared beef (#2 from Basic Sushi)
prepared eggs (#3 from Basic Sushi)
prepared crabsticks (#4 from Basic Sushi)
prepared carrots (#5 from Basic Sushi)
prepared spinach (#6 from Basic Sushi)
Place ½ sheet of nori (seaweed) on a bamboo mat*. Wet fingertips in water and evenly spread ½ cup of rice on top, leaving ½″ at the far end of the nori to seal the roll. Arrange small portions of beef, egg, crabsticks, carrots and spinach on top of the rice and, using the bamboo mat to hold the shape, roll the nori like a jellyroll. Unroll the bamboo mat and cut the roll into bite size sections using a sharp, wet knife.

◆ 계란지단 만드는 과정 (*How to make thin slice of egg fry*)

◆ 꽃다발 김밥 만드는 과정 (*How to make California Roll*)

◆ 배추연꽃 만들기
(*How to make lotus flower with cabbage*)

◆ 당근꽃 만들기
(*How to make flower with carrot*)

◆ 무우꽃 만들기 (*How to make flower with a Radish*)

◆ 막기김밥 만드는 과정 (*How to make Rolled sushi*)

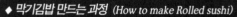

밥 · 류 (Rice dishes)

꽃다발 김밥(California Roll)

만드는 것은 이렇게

❶ 구운 김 한 장을 ¼로 잘라 4장으로 만든다. (3장−12개).
❷ 게살(4 oz)은 잘게 찢어 마요네즈 1큰술과 무치고, 아보카도 (avocado) 1개는 채썬다.
❸ 김 중간에 밥 1큰술을 놓고 ❷의 재료를 적당히 얹어 보자기 싸 듯이 중간을 고정시켜 칼로 썰면 1개가 2개 되고, 꽃다발 모양으로 김 밑부분만 감싸면 큰 꽃다발 모양 김밥이 된다.
❹ 구운 김에 밥을 쌀 때는 그 자리에서 간장에 와사비를 섞어 금방 찍어 먹어야 맛이 있다.

Making

4 oz. crabsticks (#4 from Basic Sushi) prepared rice (#1 from Basic Sushi)1 tbsp. mayonnaise toasted nori sheets* cut in quarters 1 avocado, cut in strips wasabi and soy sauce dipping mixture

Combine the crab and mayonnaise. Evenly spread one tablespoonful rice in the center of a piece of nori. Arrange the crab and avocado on top, extending out to the two opposite corners and roll diagonally. Cut the roll in the middle for two pieces. Adjust and form into a conical bouquet shape by gently squeezing the cut side. Eat this sushi right away, dipping each bite into a soy sauce and wasabi mixture.
*Available in Asian groceries.

야채 김밥(Vegetable Roll)

만드는 것은 이렇게

김 위에 1½주걱 밥을 골고루 깐 다음 상추를 판판하게 깔고 상추 위에 기본 재료 중 달걀, 당근, 시금치를 가지런히 놓고 돌돌 만다.

Making

Prepared rice (#1 from Basic Sushi), prepared eggs (#3 from Basic Sushi) prepared carrots (#5 from Basic Sushi), prepared spinach (#6 from Basic Sushi), soft lettuce leaves, nori sheets

Place a nori sheet on a bamboo mat and cover the nori with a lettuce leaf. Evenly spread ½ cup of rice on top. Arrange the remaining ingredients on the rice. Roll, using the bamboo mat to hold the shape, and cut like the rolled sushi (above).

보쌈김밥

밥 · 류 (Rice dishes)

보쌈김밥 (Boh-sahm Kim-pahp, Do It Yourself Sushi)

🍲 준비는 이렇게(4인분)

①당근채 1컵, ②오이채 1컵, ③달걀지단채 1컵, ④잔새우 1컵, ⑤게맛살 1컵(6피스를-반으로 잘라 길이로 찢음), ⑥케빌리언(Masago) 1컵, ⑦아보카도(채썬 것) 1컵, ⑧생강절임 1컵, ⑨밥(4인용 밥솥) 1솥, ⑩김(가로 19센티, 세로 20센티) 20장

🍲 만드는 것은 이렇게

❶ 재료중에서 채썬 당근만 식초 1작은술, 설탕 1큰술, 소금 ½작은술에 10분 정도 절였다가 물기를 꼭 짜면 아주 부드럽고 양념이 잘 밴다. 생강절임은 동양식품에 가공된 것이 있으므로 구입한다.

❷ 재료 ①에서 ⑦까지 색맞추어 분리된 둥근 접시에 놓고 생강절임(⑧)은 중앙에 놓는다. 다 된 밥은 따로 떠놓고 김 20장은 불에 살짝 구워 4등분으로 잘라서 식성대로 먼저 김에 밥을 놓고 고명으로 ①부터 ⑧을 골고루 놓고 보쌈해서 먹는다.

❸ 양념장은 재료를 잘 섞어서 보쌈김밥을 찍어 먹는다.

🍲 양념장은 이렇게

진간장 ⅓컵, 식초 1큰술, 정종 1큰술, 와사비 1큰술-(물 1큰술+와사비가루1큰술)

＊보쌈김밥에 쇠고기볶음, 우엉조림, 회종류(생선,튜나,광어, 문어, 조개채, 도미) 등을 채썰어 써도 색다르고 훌륭한 회보쌈이 된다.

＊밥은 쌀 4컵을 3~4번 물에 헹구어 씻고 물 4½컵을 부은 뒤 전기밥솥에 30분~40분 정도 두면 된다.

＊케빌리언(Masago)과 생강절임은 동양식품에서 구입.

🍲 4 servings

1 cup pickled ginger slices*, all liquid squeezed out, 1 tsp. vinegar, 1 tbsp. sugar, ½ tsp. salt, 1 cup carrots, thin strips marinated in vinegar, sugar and salt 10 minutes, liquid removed, 1 cup cucumber, cut in thin strips, 1 cup fried egg pancake strips, 1 cup tiny cooked shrimp, 1 cup imitation crab sticks, 6 pieces, each cut lengthwise for a total of 12 pieces, 1 cup Capelin roe (masago)*, 1 cup avocado, cut in thick slices, 4 cups rice, 20 toasted seaweed* sheets, cut each into quarters

🍲 Making

Prepare the rice in 4½ cups of water in an electric rice cooker according to the instructions. Mix the ingredients for the seasoned soy sauce.

On a large serving platter, place a clump of pickled ginger slices in the center and surround with an attractive arrangement of the remaining items, except the rice and seaweed which can be passed separately.

To enjoy, each diner places a little rice, along with as many of the other items as desired, on a piece of seaweed and dips it in the seasoned soy sauce.

🍲 For seasoned soy sauce

⅓cup soy sauce, 1 tbsp. water to mix with wasabi powder, 1 tbsp. rice wine, 1 tbsp. wasabi powder, 1 tbsp. vinegar

＊Note : Fillings can be varied; try stir-fried beef or prepared burdock root dish (see separate recipe) or any fresh raw fish, octopus or shellfish to make sashimi sushi.

＊Available in Asian groceries.

모듬초밥(Assorted Seafood Sushi)

🥢 준비는 이렇게(8인분)

쌀 4컵, 물 4½컵, 설탕 1½큰술, 식초 1큰술, 소금 ⅓작은술, 와사비 ½큰술, 생강절임 ⅓컵, 초밥용 마요네즈소스 1큰술, 김 1장

🥢 밥 만드는 것은 이렇게

❶ 쌀은 4, 5번 물에 헹구어 4컵의 쌀에 물 4½컵을 붓고 전기밥솥에 30분 정도 두어 밥을 짓는다.

❷ 다 된 밥에 삼배초 (설탕 1½큰술, 식초 1큰술, 소금, ⅓작은술) 를 잘 배합하여 밥이 뜨거울 때 섞어놓는다.

❸ 삼배초 섞은 밥을 1½큰술 떠서 손바닥에 놓고 조물조물 손가락으로 직사각형 모양(가로 1인치, 세로 2인치, 두께 0.5인치)으로 밥을 빚어 놓는다.

❹ 마요네즈소스를 손가락으로 묻혀 밥 위에 바른다.

🥢 초밥 만드는 것은 이렇게

❶ 횟감용 생선은 물에 씻지 않는다. 깨끗한 종이타월로 적당히 눌러 물기를 뺀 뒤에 가로 1.25인치, 세로 2.25인치의 크기로 자른 튜나, 연어, 도미, 방어, 삶아놓은 문어를 빚어놓은 밥 위에 올려 놓는다.

❷ 삶아놓은 새우는 배를 벌려 판판하게 칼집을 넣고 꽁지는 그냥 둔 채 밥 위에 놓는다. 횟감오징어도 밥 크기와 같이 잘라 밥 위에 올리고, 게맛살은 가로로 옆을 벌려 밥 위에 놓고 중간에 김(가로 0.5인치, 세로 3인치) 으로 테를 돌린다.

❸ 스칼롭, 미루가이, 빨간피조개는 모양대로 넓게 펴서 밥 위에 올린다.

❹ 포장과 양념이 된 장어 1마리(3oz./85g)를 칼로 가로 1.5인치, 세로 2.5인치 정도의 크기로 썰어 장어 소스를 생선 위에 붓으로 발라 오븐 브로일에 굽는다.

❺ 2분 정도 구운 뒤 생선 위에 한번 더 소스를 바르고 1분 뒤에 꺼낸 다음 밥 위에 올리고 김테(밴드)를 두른다. (1마리가 12피스 정도 됨) 살몬알, 우니, MASAGO는 알을 그냥 밥 위에 올리면 흘러내리므로 김(가로 1인치, 세로 5.5인치)으로 밥을 양옆으로 둘러싼 다음 밥이 보이는 위에 살몬알로 채우고, 우니알도 같은 모양으로 올리고 MASAGO도 밥위에 덮어 올린다.

🥢 양념장은 이렇게

진간장 3큰술, 식초 1큰술, 와사비 ½큰술

＊만들어 놓은 모든 것을 큰 접시에 색색이 모양있게 담고 간장, 식초, 와사비초장으로 초밥을 찍어먹는다.
＊와사비 배합비율 : 가루와사비 1큰술에 물 1큰술을 넣고 잘 젓는다.
＊장어소스, 생강절임은 동양식품에서 구입할 수 있음.
＊문어도 삶은 것을 동양식품에서 구입 할 수 있음.
＊식성에 따라 위에 열거한 생선 중에서 먹고 싶어하는 생선만 해도 된다.

🥢 생선 종류

튜나(참치), 연어, 도미, 방어, 문어, 새우, 오징어, 게맛살, 스칼롭, 미루가이, 빨간피조개, 장어, 살몬알, 우니, CAPELIN ROE(MASAGO)

🥢 8 servings

4 cups rice cooked in an electric rice cooker with 4½ cups water for 30 minutes, ⅓ tsp. salt (considered one of the Basic Three Ingredients), 1 tbsp. vinegar (considered one of the Basic Three Ingredients), 1½ tbsp. sugar (considered one of the Basic Three Ingredients),1 tbsp. Mayonnaise Sauce for Sushi*, 1 sheet seaweed, cut in ½″ x 3″ strips & 1″ x 5½″ strips, ⅓ cup pickled ginger slices* (Japanese brand)

🥢 Making

Put rice in a large bowl and gently, thoroughly mix in the Basic Three Ingredients. Let cool completely. Using a wet hand, form 1½ tablespoons rice into a 1″ x 2″ x ½″ thick rectangular pads and dab on some Mayonnaise Sauce with a finger tip. Repeat this with the remaining rice, making as many sushi as you want. Prepare the different kinds:

Place a slice of tuna, salmon, flounder, yellow tail, squid, octopus, scallop, clams and a shrimp on rice pads as desired.

For roe sushi, wrap a long seaweed strip around the perimeter of a rice pad, extending it about ½″ higher than the rice. Fill the top with a different roe, salmon, sea urchin or capelin. For crab sushi, place an imitation crab slice on a rice pad, wrap a short strip of seaweed around it like a belt, tucking it into itself to secure.

For eel sushi, brush eel pieces with prepared eel sauce and broil for 2 minutes. Brush each again, broil another minute, then place some eel on top of a rice pad. Band with a seaweed strip just like the crab sushi. Arrange the various sushi items colorfully on a serving platter. Place a finger squeezed clump of pickled ginger slices along side, and serve with the dipping sauce.

🥢 For dipping sauce, mix

3 tbsp. soy sauce, 1 tbsp. rice vinegar*, ½ tbsp. wasabi *

🥢 For fish, use

fresh raw tuna, cut into thin slices (1¼″ x 2¼″), fresh raw salmon fillet, cut the same as tuna, fresh raw flounder fillet, cut the same as tuna, fresh raw yellow tail fillet, cut the same as tuna, fresh raw squid* (sashimi quality), cut the same as tuna, cooked octopus tentacles*, sliced, each slice big enough to cover a rice piece, fresh scallops, slit open, each slice big enough to cover a rice piece, cooked giant clam*, sliced, each slice big enough to cover a rice piece, cooked red clam*, sliced, each slice big enough to cover a rice piece, fresh sea urchin roe*, salmon roe*, fresh, or if frozen, thawed, capelin roe* (masago), fresh, or if frozen, thawed, shrimp, cooked, tail intact, cut lengthwise from belly, opened flat (as a butterfly), imitation crab sticks*, butterfly lengthwise, cut in 2¼″ long pieces, prepared eel*, a 3 oz. package yields (10-12) 2½″ long pieces, prepared sauce for eel*

＊Note : For wasabi paste, mix a 1:1 ratio of wasabi powder and water.
＊Available in Asian groceries.

팔색미역냉채나물

팔색미역냉채나물 (Colorful Seaweed Salad)

준비는 이렇게(8인분)

마른미역 1oz., (식초 3큰술, 설탕 4큰술), 통조림 골뱅이(7.76oz), 홍합 ½ lb., 새우 20마리 정도, 게살 ½ lb., 피클용오이 7개, 당근(중간크기) 3개, 양파(중간크기) 1개, 캬베츠 ¼, 양장피 2장, 지단(계란 2개)

만드는 것은 이렇게

❶ 마른 미역을 물에 20분 이상 불린 후 깨끗이 씻어 먹기 좋은 크기로 썰어 식초 3큰술, 설탕 3큰술을 넣고 잘 주물러 냉장고 에 넣어둔다.

❷ 골뱅이는 먹기 좋은 크기로 납작하게 썰고 홍합도 잘 장만하 여 2등분씩 썰고 게맛살도 잘게 찢어놓고 당근, 양파, 캬베츠 도 채썰어 각각 설탕 1큰술, 식초 1큰술에 재운 뒤에 꼭짠다. 오이는 채썰고 지단도 잘 썰어 놓는다.

❸ 판판한 접시에 색맞추어 골고루 담고 먹기 전에 양념장, 볶음 고추장, 참기름, 볶은깨를 잘 혼합하여 재료와 함께 무쳐낸다.

＊양장피 2장은 물(3컵)이 팔팔 끓을때 넣고 불을 끄고 10분 내지 20분 지난 뒤에 불어오르면 찬물에 3, 4번 헹군 뒤 먹기좋게 찢어 놓는다.

양념장 준비는 이렇게

볶음고추장 3큰술, 참기름 3큰술, 볶은 참깨 3큰술, 식초 3큰술, 설탕 4큰술

〈당근, 캬베츠 절임용 삼배초〉: 설탕 4큰술, 식초 3큰술, 소금 1작은술

8 servings

1 oz. dried seaweed, softened in water, cut into bite size pieces, 3 tbsp.vinegar, 4 tbsp. sugar, 1 can conch (7.76 oz. already cooked), cut into bite size slices., 20 shrimp, cooked, ½ lb. mussels, cooked, each cut in half, 3 medium carrots, cut in strips, ¼ medium cabbage, cut in strips, 1 medium onion, sliced, 7 pickling cucumbers, cut in strips, 2 eggs

Making

Marinate the seaweed in the vinegar and sugar and refrigerate. Marinate the carrots in half the marinade mix for 30 minutes, then gently squeeze out the liquid. Repeat the process, using the other half of the marinade mix with the cabbage. Lightly beat the eggs with a fork and pour in a heated, greased frying pan, tilting the pan to spread the egg evenly and make a thin pancake. Turn the egg over, cook a few seconds more, then cut into strips.
Combine the dressing ingredients. Arrange the eight items attractively on a serving platter and, at the table, toss with the dressing and serve.

Marinade mix for carrots and cabbage

1 tsp. salt, 4 tbsp. sugar, 3 tbsp. vinegar

For dressing

3 tbsp. seasoned hot chili paste*, 3 tbsp. sesame oil, 3 tbsp. toasted sesame seeds.

＊Available in Asian groceries.

오색모듬말이 (Five Color Rolls)

준비는 이렇게(8인분)

배춧잎 12장 – (가로 5인치, 세로 7인치), 물 2컵, 삶은 시금치 ½컵, 우엉(고보) 1.76 oz., 게맛살 ½ lb., 통조림 유부 10장, 달걀 5개, 깻잎 8장, 김 2장, 횟감 오징어 6조각, 식용유 2큰술, 참기름 1큰술, 소금 ¾작은술

만드는 것은 이렇게

❶ 판판한 냄비에 물 2컵을 붓고 팔팔 끓을 때 배추잎을 1장씩 넣어 앞뒤로 뒤적인 다음 차곡차곡 건져낸다.(물기를 짜놓는다)

❷ 시금치는 깨끗이 씻어 팔팔 끓는 물에 살짝 데쳐낸 뒤 잘 씻어 물기를 꼭 짜고 소금 ½작은술, 참기름 1큰술 넣고 무친다.

❸ 우엉(고보)은 양념된 가공제품(일본제 Hana Brand)을 구입하여 물기만 뺀다. 게맛살은 물기를 꼭 짜고 잘 찢어놓는다.

❹ 통조림유부는 자루모양으로 된 것을 양쪽을 잘라 판판하게 직사각형으로 만든다.

❺ 달걀은 황백을 같이하여 소금 ¼작은술을 넣고 잘 저은 후 프라이팬에 식용유 2큰술을 넣고 3장 정도 부친다. 깻잎은 잘 씻어 놓는다.

❻ 김은 한 장을 4등분하여 4장 되게 잘라놓는다.

❼ 횟감용 오징어는 물기를 꼭 눌러짜고 닦아놓는다.

5가지(오색)말이 만들기

⊙ 배춧잎 : 배춧잎 2장을 겹쳐놓고, 시금치 3~4잎, 우엉(고보) 1개, 게맛살 약간 넣고 돌돌 말아 싼 뒤 한입 크기(0.8인치 정도)로 썰어 그릇에 담는다.

⊙ 유부말이 : 잘 펴놓은 유부위에 깻잎 1장을 놓고 시금치, 우엉, 게맛살을 차례로 각각 얹어 돌돌 만다.

⊙ 달걀 : 지단 부쳐놓은 달걀 위에 깻잎을 놓고 시금치, 우엉, 게맛살을 차례로 각각 얹어 돌돌 만다.

⊙ 횟감오징어 : 횟감오징어를 먼저 놓고 잘라놓은 김을 놓고 게맛살을 조금 놓고 돌돌 만다.

⊙ 깻잎말이 : 깻잎에 김을 놓고 게맛살, 시금치, 우엉을 각각 얹고 돌돌 만다.

위의 5가지 말이가 다 준비되면 0.8인치 크기로 썰어 줄맞추어 접시에 담아낸다. 양념장을 잘 혼합하여 찍어 먹는다.

＊경우에 따라서 배춧잎 모듬말이 속에 다른 재료를 넣을수도 있다.
＊우엉, 횟감오징어는 동양식품점에서 구입할 수 있음.

양념장 준비는 이렇게

진간장 3큰술, 설탕 2큰술, 식초 1큰술, 잣가루 1큰술

8 servings

12 Napa cabbage leaves, upper green portions only (5″ x 7″ each), 2 cups water, 40-50 spinach leaves, rinsed, ½ tsp. salt, 1 tbsp. sesame oil, 1.76oz. burdock root (commercially prepared Japanese Hana brand) liquid squeezed out, ½ lb. imitation crabsticks, excess moisture patted out, hand torn lengthwise., 10 seasoned fried bean curd sheets, canned, cut pocket shape open for a flat sheet., ¼ tsp. salt, 2 tbsp. cooking oil, 5 eggs, lightly beaten, salted and fried in a skillet to make 3 very thin pancakes., 8 perrila leaves* (kaht-nip), rinsed and patted dry, 2 seaweed sheets, cut into quarters, 6 fresh squid pieces, skinless, thoroughly patted dry

Making

One by one, quickly blanch each cabbage leaf in 2 cups boiling water and gently squeeze out any liquid. Dip-blanch spinach in boiling water, rinse in cold water and gently squeeze out excess liquid. Season with ½ teaspoon salt and 1 tablespoon sesame oil. Combine the seasoned soy sauce ingredients. Prepare the five color rolls per below.
Napa cabbage leaf rolls · Spread and overlap two leaves to make a large sheet. Stack 3-4 spinach leaves, a piece of burdock root, some crabsticks and roll up like a jellyroll.
Fried bean curd rolls: On each bean curd sheet, lay one perrila leaf, some spinach, burdock root and crabsticks and roll up.

Egg pancake rolls : Follow the same process as the fried bean curd roll.
Fresh squid rolls : On a piece of squid, put some seaweed and crabsticks and roll up.
Perilla leaf rolls : Cover each leaf with some spinach, burdock root, crabsticks and roll up.
Cut each kind of roll into approximately ¾″ bite size pieces and arrange colorfully on a platter. Serve with the seasoned soy sauce.

For seasoned soy sauce

3 tbsp. soy sauce, 2 tbsp. sugar, 1 tbsp. vinegar, 1 tbsp. crushed pine nuts

＊Available in Asian groceries.

1   2   3   4

겨자채 (Seafood Salad with Mustard Dressing)

🍲 준비는 이렇게(15인분)

중간새우(삶은 것) 40마리, 오징어 1마리, 맛게살(8센티 길이) 12피스, 달걀 3개, 불린표고버섯 3장, 씨없는 오이 1개, 캬베츠 ¼쪽, 당근 5개, 양장피 4장 (5oz.), 식용유 2큰술

🍲 만드는 것은 이렇게

❶ 중간새우는 쿠킹된 것으로 한번 씻어 물기를 뺀다. 껍질이 있으면 벗겨놓는다.

❷ 오징어는 몸만 껍질을 벗기고 판판한 냄비에 물 2컵을 붓고 팔팔 끓을 때 살짝 데쳐낸다. 식으면 채썰어 놓는다.

❸ 게맛살 12피스는 잘게 잘 찢어 놓는다.

❹ 달걀 3개는 잘 풀어서 판판한 프라이팬에 식용유 1큰술을 붓고 뜨거운 느낌이 있을 때 2장 정도 지단을 지져놓는다. 약간 식으면 채썬다.

❺ 3시간 이상 불린 표고버섯은 꼭지를 떼어내고 채썰어 물기를 꼭 짜고 판판한 프라이팬에 식용유 1큰술을 붓고 볶아놓는다.

❻ 씨없는 오이는 잘 씻어 껍질째로 채썰어 놓는다.

❼ 둥근 캬베츠는 4등분한 한쪽을 속의 굵은심을 빼고 곱게 채 썰어 놓는다. 삼배초(설탕 2큰술, 식초 1½큰술, 소금 ½작은술)에 30분 동안 숨을 죽인 다음 간이 밴 캬베츠를 꼭 잡아 물기를 뺀다.

❽ 당근 5개는 껍질을 벗기고 채썰어 설탕 3큰술, 식초 2큰술, 소금 ½작은술을 넣고 30분정도 숨을 죽이면 부드럽고 색깔이 더욱 아름답다. 물기를 꼭 짜놓는다.

❾ 양장피 4장은 판판하고 오목한 중간냄비에 물 5컵을 붓고 팔팔 끓을 때 적당히 4등분 손으로 부셔넣고 2분정도 뒤에 양장피가 끓으면 불을 끄고 그 냄비 그대로 30분 이상 뚜껑을 닫고 기다렸다가 열어보면 파들파들하게 2배 이상 부풀어 있다. 이때 채에 받쳐 찬물에 몇번 헹군 뒤 먹기좋게 손으로 뜯어놓고 물기를 뺀다.

❿ 위의 모든 재료가 준비되면 큼직하고 판판한 접시에 색맞추어 골고루 담고 야채는 바깥쪽으로 하고 중간 공간에는 양장피를 담고 중앙 윗부분에 새우를 담으면 색이 아름답고 예술품 요리접시가 된다.

🍲 양념장 준비는 이렇게

와사비 1큰술(물1큰술+가루와사비1큰술), 참기름 3큰술, 후추 ½작은술, 볶은통깨 2큰술, 설탕 3큰술, 식초 3큰술, 파 1쪽(다짐), 다진마늘 1큰술, 스시용 마요네즈 ⅓컵(일본제품)

○ 양념장을 분량대로 잘 혼합하여 ⑩에 붓고 먹기 전에 골고루 섞어 상에 낸다.

＊ 큰 접시에 더욱 모양있게 놓고 싶은 분은 야채의 재료(오이,당근,캬베츠,표고버섯,지단)와 해물(오징어,맛게살)을 똑같은 크기로 끝을 단발머리 깎듯이 깡충 줄세워 잘라 흐트러짐 없이 색맞추어 접시에 담고 공간 중간 부분에 양장피를 돌려가며 깔고 맨 위에 새우를 놓는다.

＊ 양장피 대신 삶은 흰 당면을 써도 맛이 좋다.

🍲 15 servings

40 shrimp, cooked, shelled, rinsed and dried, 1 squid (body only), skinless, blanched in boiling water, rinsed, cut in thin strips, 12 imitation crab sticks, each 3″ long, shredded lengthwise by hand, 3 eggs, lightly beaten with a fork, fried into paper-thin pancakes, cut in thin strips., 3 black mushrooms, softened in water, liquid squeezed out, cut in thin strips , 1 cucumber, seedless or seeded and cut in thin strips, ¼ cabbage, cored, cut in thin strips, 5 carrots, peeled, cut in thin strips 4 mungbean starch sheets : water as needed

🍲 Making

Combine the Basic Three Ingredients. Marinate the cabbage in half this mixture for 30 minutes or until wilted, then gently squeeze out the liquid. Marinate the carrots in the other half of the Basic Three Ingredients mixture for 30 minutes or until wilted, then gently squeeze out any liquid. Stir-fry the mushrooms in a heated, oiled fry pan.
Cook the mungbean starch sheets in 5 cups boiling water for 2 minutes, remove from heat, cover and let stand for 30 minutes until they swell to double their size. Rinse in cold water, hand tear into bite sized pieces, then drain thoroughly.
Mix the mustard dressing ingredients. In the center of a serving platter, place the mungbean starch sheets with the seafood pieces on the top. Colorfully arrange the vegetables around the rim. At the table, toss with the mustard dressing and enjoy.

🍲 For the Basic Three Ingredients

4 tbsp. sugar, 2 tbsp. vinegar, 1 tsp. salt

🍲 For mustard dressing

1 tbsp. wasabi powder, 3 tbsp. sesame oil, 1 tbsp. water, 1 tsp. black pepper, 2 tbsp. toasted sesame seeds, 3 tbsp. sugar, 3 tbsp. vinegar, 1 tbsp. spring onion, chopped, 1 tbsp. garlic, minced, ⅓ cup mayonnaise sauce for sushi

＊Notes : To create a different look, cut all the ingredients, except the shrimp and mungbean sheets, to the same length. Put the mungbean sheets in the middle with shrimp on top and arrange the rest colorfully and neatly around the rim.
Transparent noodles can be substituted for mungbean starch sheets.

1　　　　2　　　　3　　　　4

잡채

잡채 (Transparent Noodles with Vegetables)

준비는 이렇게(6인분)

당면 7.75 oz.(220g), 삶은 시금치 5oz, 불린표고버섯 2장, 불린 목이버섯 1½ 컵, 양파 1개, 당근(중간크기) 1½, 배추줄기 잎 2장, 캬베츠(채썰어) ½ cup, 쇠고기 0.3 lb., 진간장 2큰술, 물 2 Ltr.

만드는 것은 이렇게

❶ 물 2 Ltr.를 냄비에 넣고 팔팔 끓을때 당면(7.75 oz)을 넣어 삶는다.

❷ 젓가락으로 골고루 붙지 않게 잘 저으면서 3분 정도 지나 윤기가 반짝반짝 나면 찬물에 국수채반을 놓고 차게 헹구어낸다.

❸ 물기가 빠지면 먹기좋은 크기로 가위로 듬성듬성 자른다.

❹ 당면에 진간장 2큰술을 넣고 당면과 간장을 버무리면 브라운 색으로 변한다.

❺ 납작한 프라이팬에 불을 켜고 식용유 2큰술을 넣고 자작자작 할 때 물든 당면을 넣고 볶는다. 센불에 4~5분 볶으면 당면 색깔이 똑같고 반짝반짝 윤기가 난다.

❻ 볶은 당면을 판판한 그릇에 식힌다. 쇠고기는 채썰어 불고기 양념을 한 다음 프라이팬에 볶는다.

❼ 3시간 이상 물에 불린 버섯 2종류 잘 씻어 물기를 빼고 표고버섯 채썬 것과 목이버섯도 식용유 1큰술 넣고 2분 정도 볶는다.

❽ 채썰어 놓은 양파, 당근, 배추 줄기, 캬베츠도 식용유 1큰술 넣고 1분 정도 볶는다. 야채들을 볶을 때 소금과 마늘가루 ½ 작은술을 약간 뿌린다.

❾ 삶은 시금치는 그냥 쓴다. 준비된 당면과 쇠고기,야채들을 판판한 그릇에 담고 마지막 양념을 한다. 볶은깨, 참기름, 후추, 진간장, 설탕을 분량대로 넣고 잘 버무려 상에 낼 때 위에 지단을 뿌리고 쑥갓이 있으면 드문드문 위에 올려낸다.

양념장 준비는 이렇게

볶은깨 2큰술, 참기름 2½큰술, 설탕 1½큰술, 후추 ½ 작은술, 진간장 2큰술, 식용유 4큰술, 소금마늘가루 ½작은술, 달걀 1개

* 계절에 따라 부추를 넣으면 부추잡채, 풋고추를 볶아 넣으면 풋고추 잡채가 됨. 버섯은 양송이를 써도 된다.

* 주의할 점 : 잡채는 모든 재료의 온도가 똑같아야 변하지 않음.

6 servings

7.75 oz. transparent noodles, 2 liters water, 2 tbsp. dark soy sauce, 1 onion, sliced, 1 medium carrot, cut in thin strips, 2 Napa cabbage leaves, white stalks only, ½ cup cabbage, shredded, 2 black mushrooms, softened in water and cut into this strips, 1½ cups woodear* mushroom, softened in water, torn in bite sizes, ⅓ lb. beef, cut into thin strips and marinated in Boul Ko-ki sauce (recipe 21), 5 oz. spinach leaves, blanched and gently squeezed, 4 tbsp. cooking oil, garlic salt and salt, fried egg pancake strips for garnish

Making

Cook the noodles in boiling water until transparent, about 3 minutes, then rinse in cold water, drain and cut into 3-5″ pieces. Thoroughly mix the dark soy sauce into the noodles. Heat 2 tablespoons of oil in a skillet. Stir-fry the noodles for 4-5 minutes until evenly dark and shiny and remove to a wide mixing bowl to cool.

Combine the seasoning ingredients. Set aside.

Using ½ teaspoon of oil and a sprinkling of salt and garlic salt each time, individually stir-fry for 1 minute, in order, the onion, carrot, Napa cabbage leaves, cabbage, mushrooms and finally the beef. Allow each of these to cool to room temperature and then combine these ingredients with the spinach and transparent noodles. Finish by adding the seasoning mix to taste. Garnish with fried egg strips.

For seasoning

2 tbsp. toasted sesame seeds, 2½ tbsp. sesame oil, 1½ tsps. black pepper, 1½ tbsp. sugar, 2 tbsps. dark soy sauce

* Note : Seasonal vegetables such as garlic chives or chilies can create tasty variations. The temperatures of all ingredients should be about the same when combined to preserve the natural colors and retard spoilage.

별 · 미 · 요 · 리 (Specials)

양장피 잡채 (Salad with Mungbean Starch Sheet)

🍲 준비는 이렇게(8~10인분)

쇠고기 ¼ lb., 새우 ½ lb., 게살 ½ lb., 어묵 ½, 불린표고버섯 50g, 목이버섯 50g, 송이버섯 50g, 씨없는 긴 오이 1개 정도, 당근 4개 정도, 지단 1장 (달걀 2개), 양파 중간 것 2개, 파 1단, 양장피 4장, 식용유 3큰술

🍲 만드는 것은 이렇게

❶ 양장피는 팔팔 끓는 물에 삶고 10분~20분 지난 뒤에 찬물에 헹구어 먹기 좋은 크기로 찢어 식용유 1큰술에 살짝 볶는다.

❷ 새우는 쿠킹된 것으로 껍질이 있으면 벗겨 한번 씻어 물기를 빼두고 게살은 잘게 찢어놓는다.

❸ 새우와 게살을 제외한 모든 재료를 적당한 크기의 채로 썰어 (쇠고기, 어묵, 3가지 버섯, 오이, 당근, 양파, 파) 소금과 마늘가루를 조금씩 뿌려가면서 식용유 2큰술에 다 함께 살짝 볶아 놓는다.

❹ 지단도 채썰어 판판하고 큰 그릇에 위의 재료들을 다 놓고 만들어 놓은 양념장을 섞어 무쳐서 상에 낸다.

❋ 색 맞추어 접시에 골고루 담고 양념장을 뿌려 낸다.

🍲 양념장 준비는 이렇게

겨자 1큰술, 마늘 다진것 1½큰술, 생강 다진것 1큰술, 후추 ½작은술 볶은깨 2큰술, 쇠고기 국물 1컵(육수), 설탕 1큰술, 참기름 3큰술, 소금 ½작은술

🍲 8~10 servings

¼ lb. beef, cut in thin strips, ½ lb. shrimp, 4 mungbean starch sheets* 12″ diameter (Pun-Fay in Chinese), cooked, ½ lb. crab flavored fish cake, , ½ kamaboko* fish cake, sliced (comes on a wooden board), 50g black mushrooms, softened in water and cut in thin strips, 10 dried woodear mushrooms, softened in water and torn into bite sized pieces, 10 fresh mushrooms (button mushrooms), sliced, 1 cucumber, cut in thin strips, 4 carrots, cut in thin strips, 2 medium onions, thinly sliced, 6 spring onions, cut in thin strips, 2 eggs, corn oil or sesame oil for stir-frying, salt and pepper to season

🍲 Making

Cook the mungbean starch sheets in boiling water for a few minutes and let stand in the water for 10-20 minutes. Rinse in cold water, drain and tear into bite size pieces. Using a little oil and sprinkling with salt and pepper, briefly stir-fry each of the following: the mungbean starch sheets, shrimp, beef, each variety of mushroom, the cucumbers, carrots, onions and spring onions. (In between each ingredient, wipe the frying pan clean with a paper towel to preserve the ingredient's color.)

Beat the eggs with a fork and pour into a hot, greased frying pan, tilt the pan to spread the eggs evenly, making a thin pancake. Cut the cooked egg into thin strips.

Combine the dressing ingredients and mix thoroughly. Arrange the salad colorfully on a serving platter. At the table, toss the salad with the dressing and serve.

🍲 For the dressing

1tbsp. prepared hot mustard, 1 tbsp. ginger, finely grated, 1½ tbsp garlic, minced, ½ tsp. black pepper, 2 tbsp. sesame seeds, toasted, 1 tbsp. sugar, ½ tsp. salt, 1 cup beef broth, 3 tbsp. sesame oil

❋ Available in Asian groceries

두부명란젓찜(Bean Curd with Fish Roe)

준비는 이렇게(1인분)

양념된 명란젓 ½컵, 물 ½컵, 두부 ½모, 후추 ¼작은술, 달걀흰자 1개, 파 1뿌리

만드는 것은 이렇게

명란젓을 잘게 자른 후 물 ½컵을 뚝배기에 붓고 같이 넣어 팔팔 끓을 때 으깬 두부를 넣고 또다시 끓을 때 달걀 흰자만 풀어넣고 또 끓을 때 후추와 파를 잘게 다져 넣고 상에 낸다.

*처음부터 시간이 얼마 걸리지 않으므로 계속 저으면서 밑이 눋지 않도록 한다. (아주 영양가 높고 별미임)

I serving

½ cup seasoned pollack roe*, cut in ½″ long pieces, ½ cup water, ½ lb. bean curd, coarsely broken with a fork, ¼ tsp.salt, 1 egg white, lightly beaten with fork, 1 spring onion, chopped

Making

In a small saucepan, combine the water and pollack roe and bring to a boil. Add the bean curd and black pepper. Stir in the egg white and spring onion. Serve at once.

*Notes : This cooks very quickly and must be closely watched.
Enjoy this dish for its high nutrition and unique flavor.

*Available in Asian groceries.

(별) · 미 · 요 · 리 (Specials)

두부고추장 볶음(Spicy Bean Curd)

🍲 준비는 이렇게(4인분)

두부 큰 것 2모, 돼지고기 or 쇠고기 ½ lb., 파 1뿌리, 마늘 3쪽, 생강 조금(납작하게 썬 것 4쪽), 붉은 고추 1개, 완두 2큰술, 녹말가루 2작은술 , 물 2½작은술, 간장 2큰술, 고추장 1½큰술, 설탕 ½큰술, 육수 ½ 컵, 식용유 1큰술

🍲 만드는 것은 이렇게

❶ 두부는 사방 2 센티 되게 썰어 끓는 소금물에 데쳐 물기를 뺀다.

❷ 돼지고기나 쇠고기는 살고기를 골라 채썰어 둔다. 파, 마늘, 생강을 깨끗이 다듬어 곱게 채썰고 붉은 고추도 채썬 후 씨는 전부 골라 버린다.

❸ 완두콩은 소금물에 살짝 데친다. 두꺼운 프라이팬을 달구어 식 용유를 넣고 파, 마늘, 생강, 붉은 고추를 넣고 볶다가 돼지고기 (혹은 쇠고기)를 넣어 함께 볶는다.

❹ 고기가 다 익으면 간장, 고추장, 설탕, 육수를 붓고 끓도록 놓 아둔다.

❺ 한참 끓을 때 두부를 부서지지 않도록 넣고 녹말가루를 물에 개어 부어 걸쭉하게 익힌다.

❻ 불에서 내리기 전에 완두콩을 넣고 살살 조심성있게 젓는다.

🍲 4 servings

2 pieces large bean curd, cut into ¾″ cubes, ½ lb. beef (or pork), cut into thin strips, 1 spring onion, cut into thin strips, 3 cloves garlic, sliced, 4 slices ginger, sliced, 1 red chili, remove seeds and cut into thin strips, ½ cup broth, 2 tbsp. soy sauce, 1½ tbsp. hot chili paste*, ½ tbsp. sugar, 2 tsp. cornstarch, 2 tbsp. peas, cooked and seasoned with salt, cooking oil for stir-frying, salted water

🍲 Making

Blanch the bean curd in salted boiling water, drain and remove excess liquid. In a heavy skillet, heat a little cooking oil and stir-fry spring onion, garlic, ginger and red chili. Then add the beef or pork. When the meat is cooked, add broth, soy sauce, hot chili paste and sugar and bring to a boil. Carefully add the bean curd and thicken with cornstarch mixed with a little water. Before removing from heat, carefully stir in the peas.

＊ Available in Asian groceries.

별 · 미 · 요 · 리 (Specials)

두부구이 (Pan-Fried Bean Curd)

🍲 준비는 이렇게(3인분)

두부 1모, 식용유 2½큰술

🍲 만드는 것은 이렇게

❶ 두부를 2등분하고 두께 ½인치, 넓이 2인치, 길이 2½인치로 (두부 1모가 12피스 정도 되게) 썰어 물기를 뺀 후 프라이팬에 기름을 두르고 약간 달아오르면 두부를 판판히 놓고 노릇노릇 지진다.

❷ 기름과 물이 섞이면 튀어나오므로 적당히 뚜껑을 열었다 닫았다하면서 굽는다.

❸ 두부에 불을 끄면서 양념장 재료를 잘 섞어 두부 위에 골고루 뿌린다.

❹ 양념장을 다 끼얹은 뒤 불을 한번 더 켜서(30초 정도)잘잘 소리날 때 접시에 담는다.

🍲 양념장 준비는 이렇게

참기름 2큰술, 진간장 2½큰술, 볶은 통깨 1큰술, 다진파 ⅓컵, 고춧가루 ½큰술, 다진마늘 1큰술

＊두부 위의 고명으로 잣이나 황 · 백 지단, 당근(꽃모양), 봄철엔 쑥갓잎 등을 뿌리면 한층 돋보인다.

🍲 3 servings

1 lb. bean curd, cut 2″ x 2½″ x ½″ thick into about 12 pieces, patted dry, 2½ tbsp. cooking oil

🍲 Making

In a skillet, heat oil and fry both sides of the bean curd until lightly browned, adjust the lid to avoid splatters. Remove the pan from the burner.

Combine the ingredients for the seasoned soy sauce and add to the pan. Return the pan to the burner and cook until it sizzles, about 30 seconds.

🍲 For seasoned soy sauce

2 tbsp. sesame oil, 2½ tbsp. soy sauce, 1 tbsp. toasted sesame seeds, ½ tsp. hot chili powder*, ⅓ cup spring onion, chopped, 1 tbsp. minced garlic

＊Note : For an appetizing presentation, garnish with pine nuts, white and yellow egg strips, flower shaped carrot slices or sue-kaht* (edible chrysanthemum leaves).

＊Available in Asian groceries.

별 · 미 · 요 · 리 (Specials)

어묵떡볶이 (Fried Fishcake with Rice Cake)

🍲 준비는 이렇게(4인분)

오뎅 ½ Pkg., 떡볶이 떡 ½ Pkg(1 lb.), 캬베츠(중간크기) ¼ 개, 양송이 버섯 10개 정도

🍲 만드는 것은 이렇게

❶ 떡은 물에 2시간 정도 담가 놓는다.
❷ 오뎅은 적당한 크기로 썬다.(세로 2인치, 가로 1인치 정도) 캬 베츠도 적당한 크기로 썬다. 넓은 냄비에 물 3컵과 간장, 고추 장, 고춧가루, 설탕, 마늘을 넣고 끓인다.
❸ 양념소스가 끓으면 오뎅을 넣고 한번 더 끓인 다음 버섯과 캬베츠, 떡을 넣고 끓이다 소금으로 간한다.

🍲 양념장 준비는 이렇게

고춧가루 ½작은술, 고추장 1큰술, 설탕 1큰술, 다진 마늘 1작은술, 진간장 1큰술, 소금 약간 1작은술, 물 3컵

🍲 4 servings

3 cups water, 1 tbsp. soy sauce, 1 tbsp. hot chili paste*, ½ tsp. hot chili powder*, 1 tbsp. sugar, 1 tsp. minced garlic, ½ pkg. fried fishcake*, (brown in color, comes in a 3″ x 5″ x ¼″ rectangular shape), ¼ medium cabbage, cut into bite size pieces, 10 button mushrooms, cut into halves, 1 lb. steamed rice cake*, cut in 2-3″ pieces, soaked in water 2 hours, drained, 1 tsp. salt

🍲 Making

In a big saucepan, boil water with soy sauce, chili paste, chili powder, sugar and garlic.
Cut the fried fishcake into 1″ x 2″ pieces. Add these to the saucepan and bring to a boil. Then add the mushrooms, cabbage and rice cake. When this boils again, season with salt.

*Available in Asian groceries.

떡볶이

떡볶이 (Stir-fried Rice Cake, Deukbokki)

🍲 준비는 이렇게(4인분)

떡볶이떡 1 lb., 물 1½ 리터, 불린 표고버섯 2장, 쇠고기 ⅓ lb., 참기름 2½큰술, 파 3쪽, 식용유 2큰술, 양파(작은 것) 1개, 흑설탕 1큰술, 진간장 3큰술, 다진마늘 1작은술, 볶은통깨 1½큰술, 당근(작은 것) 1개, 달걀 1개, 잣 1작은술, 실고추 1작은술

🍲 만드는 것은 이렇게

❶ 냄비에 물 1½리터를 붓고 팔팔 끓을 때 참기름 ½작은술을 넣고 떡을 넣는다.

❷ 2분 정도 뒤에 삶은 떡을 찬물에 헹군 다음 떡을 반으로(손가락크기로) 자른다.

❸ 프라이팬에 쇠고기는 가늘게 채썰어 볶아 놓고 표고버섯도 채썰어 같이 또 볶는다.

❹ 당근, 양파도 채썰어 볶아놓는다.

❺ 마지막으로 삶아 썰어놓은 떡과 고기, 버섯, 당근, 양파를 다같이 넣어 볶다가(1분 정도) 진간장 3큰술, 볶은깨 1½큰술, 설탕 1큰술, 다진마늘 1작은술을 넣는다. 맨끝에 참기름 2큰술 넣고 파를 어슷어슷 썰어 넣고 불을 끄고 접시에 담는다.

✳ 황백지단을 각각 1큰술 뿌리고 잣을 1작은술 위에 뿌리고 상에 낸다.

✳ 실고추가 있으면 약간 뿌려도 좋다.

🍲 4 servings

1 lb. rice cake*, 1½ ltr. water, ⅓ lb. beef, cut into thin strips, 2 mushrooms, softened in water and cut into strips, 1 small onion, sliced, 1 small carrot, cut into thin strips, 2 tbsp. cooking oil, 1 tbsp. brown sugar, 3 tbsp. dark soy sauce, 1 tsp. minced garlic, 1½ tbsp. toasted sesame seeds, 3 spring onions, cut 2″ long, 2 tbsp. sesame oil garnishes: egg strips (yellow and white), pine nuts and/or shredded red chili*

🍲 Making

In a saucepan, bring water to a boil, add ½ teaspoon sesame oil and the rice cake. Cook 2 minutes, then rinse in cold water, drain in a colander and cut in 3″ lengths. In a skillet, stir-fry the beef until brown. Separately stir-fry the mushrooms, then the carrot strips and then the small onion. Combine all these and the rice cake in the same skillet and cook for a minute. Add the soy sauce, sesame seeds, sugar and garlic. Just before serving, add the sesame oil and spring onions. Garnish with egg strips, pine nuts and shredded red chili to taste.

✳ Available in Asian groceries.

PART 6

꽃게장 담그기(Pickled Crab)

준비는 이렇게(5인분)

꽃게 8마리, 물 8컵, 식초 ½컵

만드는 것은 이렇게

❶ 살아있는 꽃게 8마리를 냉동에 하룻밤을 재운 뒤 다음날 손으로 골고루 깨끗이 잡티와 찌꺼기를 제거하고 몇번이고 깨끗이 씻은 다음 살이 없는 다리 끝은 가위로 잘라내고 삼각형으로 생긴 배꼽부분을 잡아당겨 등딱지를 먼저 떼어낸 뒤 몸에 붙은 큰머리(아가미)를 분리한다.

❷ 등딱지와 아가미 떼어낸 자리에도 깨끗이 한번 더 손질한 다음, 아가미에 붙은 속을 그대로 두고 물기가 빠지게 엎어놓는다. 게의 집게발은 철갑같이 딱딱하므로 게집게 가위로 꽉 집어주면 먹기가 쉽다. 채반에 손질한 게를 담아둔다.

❸ 물 8컵을 팔팔 끓여 불을 끄면서 식초를 넣고 한번 저은 뒤 채반에 있는 게에 붓는다.

❹ 그 다음 채반을 양손에 들고 몇번 털고나면 완전히 소독되고 물기가 쫙 빠진다.

❺ 5분쯤 기다렸다 만들어 놓은 소스를 넣고 버무린다.

❻ 엎어놓은 아가미에도 양념을 조금씩 넣고 병이나 판판한 뚜껑 있는 그릇에 아가미부터 밑에 깔고 그 위에 양념한 게를 소복히 담아 꼭꼭 눌러두었다가 냉장고에 보관한다. 이틀 뒤부터 먹는다.

소스는 이렇게

고춧가루 7큰술, 소주나 정종 3큰술, 후추 1작은술, 진간장 3큰술, 오징어소스 3큰술, 다진 마늘 3큰술, 다진 생강 1큰술, 물엿 2큰술, 설탕 1큰술, 볶은깨 4큰술, 포도주 1큰술

＊게장에는 야채를 넣으면 물기가 생기므로 오래두지 못하고 지저분한 느낌이 있으므로 양념만 사용한다.

＊동양식품점에서 구입. (타일랜드 제품)

5 servings

8 small live crabs, 8 cups water, ½ cup vinegar

Making

Refrigerate the live crabs overnight. The next day scrub them with a vegetable brush until clean and snip off the end leg joints. Make an incision just at the back of the eyes and cut out the face. Pull off the top shell and reserve, along with the attached buttery parts, but remove and discard the gills and spongy parts, then gently rinse. Crack the claws and place the crabs upside down in a colander to drain.

Boil the water and vinegar and pour (a hot vinegar shower) over the crabs in the colander. Shake the colander to get rid of excess liquid and let stand for 5 minutes.

Combine all the ingredients for the pickling seasoning. With the crabs in a bowl, carefully add the pickling seasoning mixture and rub some of the seasoning inside the top shells. One by one, place the shells upside down in a container, reinsert a crab into each shell, cover tightly and refrigerate. The dish will be ready to eat in 2 days.

For pickilng seasoning

7 tbsp. hot chili powder*, 4 tbsp. rice wine or wine, 1 tsp. black pepper, 3 tbsp. soy sauce, 3 tbsp. minced garlic, 1 tbsp. grated ginger, 2 tbsp. corn syrup, 1 tbsp. sugar, 4 tbsp. toasted sesame seeds, 1 tbsp. wine, 3 tbsp. liquid from brined tiny squid*

＊Note : Vegetables are not used with this preparation as they add more liquid, thereby diluting the sauce, and adversely affect the storage life of the dish. They will also result in a rather sloppy presentation.

＊Available in Asian groceries.

별 · 미 · 요 · 리 (Specials)

약식(Steamed Sweet Rice)

🍲 준비는 이렇게(6인분)

찹쌀 2 lbs.(32oz), 대추 55개 (1컵), 흑설탕 1½컵, 참기름 1컵, 진간장 1 큰술, 통계피 6쪽, 밤 통조림 13.05oz(370g), 잣 ⅓컵

🍲 만드는 것은 이렇게

❶ 찹쌀 2 lbs.에 물을 3배 이상 붓고 6시간 이상 불린다.

❷ 불린 찹쌀을 떡시루에 보자기를 깔고 골고루 놓고 고두밥을 찐 다. 불린 대추는 통채로 칼도마에 놓고 돌려가면서 썰면 씨만 남는다. 씨는 버린다.

❸ 찹쌀이 다 쪄진 다음 판판한 그릇에 담고 대추, 흑설탕, 참기름, 진간장을 잘 섞어 버무린 뒤 통계피를 군데군데 6조각 놓고 또 찐다.

❹ 통조림밤은 먹기좋은 크기로 썰어 밥 위에 붓고 잘 저어 15분 정도 또다시 찐다.

❺ 다 된 약식은 반짝반짝하며 밥알이 하나씩 크기가 똑같고 색깔 이 완전히 똑같으면서 부드럽다.

❻ 그때 큰 그릇에 담기 전에 잣 ⅓컵을 넣고 골고루 젓는다.

❼ 계피는 걷어낸다. 꼭꼭 눌러서 사각모양으로 썰어서 쓰기도 하 고 그냥 동글동글하게 쓰기도 하고 여러 가지 모양으로 쓸 수 있다.

＊ 잘된 약식은 처음 고두밥을 찔 때 잘 쪄주면 된다.

＊ 계피는 향기를 내는 데 좋다. 가루계피를 사용할 경우 마지막에 뿌 리는데 약식의 빛깔이 반짝반짝하지 않으므로 통계피를 쓰는 것이 더 좋다.

🍲 6 servings

2 lbs. glutinous rice*, 55 dried red dates* (1 cup), pitted, quartered, 1 ½ cups brown sugar, 1 cup sesame oil, 1 tbsp. dark soy sauce, 6 cinnamon sticks, 13 oz. peeled, cooked chestnuts (370g can), cut in peanut sized pieces, ⅓ cup pine nuts

🍲 Making

Rinse the rice several times and soak in 3 times as much water for 6 hours or longer and then drain. In a steamer, lined with a wet kitchen cloth towel, steam the rice until done but not mushy (this is a very important step in making a perfect yahk-shick).

Empty the steamed rice into a large mixing bowl and thoroughly combine with the remaining ingredients, except the pine nuts, coating evenly with the soy sauce and brown sugar (another key step in making a perfect yahk-shick).

Return the mixture to the steamer lined with the same cloth and steam for 15 minutes, when the rice should look shiny, with each grain uniform in size. Empty the rice mixture into a large bowl, remove the cinnamon sticks and sprinkle with the pine nuts. Place in a square or round greased container to shape or form into patties for serving.

＊Note : Cinnamon powder can be used in place of cinnamon sticks but it must be added at the end of the preparation to retain the rice`s shiny appearance.

＊Available in Asian groceries.

별 · 미 · 요 · 리 (Specials)

마이크로 오븐찰떡 (Microwave Rice Cakes)

🍲 준비는 이렇게(8인분)

팥 12oz.(340g)×2봉지, 찹쌀가루(일본제품) 1 lb. - (16oz., 454g), 소금 약간, 당원(설탕 대용)약간, 베이킹소다 ½작은술, 소금 ½작은술, 물

🍲 팥고물 만드는 것은 이렇게

❶ 팥은 2시간 정도 미지근한 물에 담근 뒤 잘 씻어 물을 3배 이상 붓고 깊숙한 냄비에 1시간 정도 삶아낸다. (＊베이킹소다를 ½ 작은술 넣으면 빨리 됨)

❷ 다 익으면 자작자작 소리가 나면서 아주 부드럽고, 방망이로 두들기면 금방 으스러진다.

❸ 조금씩 맛을 보면서 소금을 넣고 당원을 아주 조금 넣으면 맛이 난다. 다 된 팥은 판판한 그릇에 담아 식힌다.

🍲 찹쌀떡 만드는 것은 이렇게

❶ 찹쌀가루 16oz.에 물 2컵을 넣고 잘 혼합한다. 경우에 따라 물이 좀 더 먹힐 수도 있으니 조금씩 더 넣어도 된다.(잘 된 반죽은 시멘트가루 갠 것 같이 축축하게)

❷ 뚜껑이 있는 코닝웨어에 반죽한 찹쌀을 판판히 담고 뚜껑을 덮은 후 마이크로 오븐에 8분30초 동안 가열한 다음 젓가락으로 저어보면 흰가루가 보이지 않고 반짝반짝하게 익은 떡이 된다.

❸ 판판한 그릇에 팥고물을 담고 뜨거울 때 고물을 떡 전체에 덮어놓고 가위나 칼로 손가락만큼 잘라 팥고물을 꼭꼭 묻혀 접시에 모양있게 담는다.

＊ 훌륭한 찹쌀떡이 됨.

＊ 콩고물이나 녹두고물, 흰콩고물 등 골고루 다 사용하면 변화있어 좋다.

＊당원을 쓰는 이유는 단맛을 내기 위함으로 설탕을 넣으면 파슬파슬한 맛이 없다.

🍲 8 servings

24 oz. dried red beans*(2), 12 oz. packages, ½ tsp baking soda (optional), ¼ tsp. salt, saccharine or sugar to taste, 16 oz. glutinous rice flour* (Japanese product), water, as needed

🍲 Making

Rinse, then soak the beans in 3 times their volume of lukewarm water. Two hours later, cook them in a deep saucepan for 1 hour (baking soda can be added to speed up cooking time) and remove excess liquid. Sprinkle salt and saccharine or sugar to taste over the hot beans and very lightly mash to a crumbling texture. Let cool in a flat-bottomed dish.

In a mixing bowl, combine the rice flour and 2 cups water (sometimes, needs adjusting) to make a slightly runny batter. Pour into a flat microwave-safe glass dish, cover and cook on high for $8\frac{1}{2}$ minutes in a microwave oven. It is done when no raw flour remains and it looks shiny when probed by a chop stick. While still hot, roll in and evenly coat with the prepared bean mixture and cut into bite size pieces. Be sure to coat the cut sides with the bean mixture.

＊Note : Toasted soybean powder, mungbean or any beans prepared as above can be substituted for the red bean mixture.

＊Available in Asian groceries.

별 · 미 · 요 · 리 (Specials)

오복경단떡 (Sweet Rice Dumplings)

준비는 이렇게(6인분)

찹쌀가루 1lb.(16oz/454g)−(일본제품,KodaFarms), 물 1½컵, 떡끓이는 물 20컵, 팥앙금(통조림) 1개, 케이크가루 3컵.

만드는 것은 이렇게

❶ 찹쌀가루에 물 1½컵을 붓고 잘 버무려 반죽한다.

❷ 반죽된 찹쌀을 손바닥으로 부드러워질 때까지 비벼서 반질반질해지면 떡가락같이 길게 몇등분 만들어 놓고 하나씩 사방 3센티 정도로 떼어서 송편 빚듯이 양손가락으로 조물조물 얇은 동그라미(사방 8센티 정도의 크기)로 만든다. 팥앙금을 넣고 오므려 속이 보이지 않게 동그라미를 만든다.

❸ 5개 정도씩 만들 때마다 20컵의 끓는 물에 넣는다.

❹ 다 익으면, 경단이 물 위로 뜰 때 건져내어 준비해놓은 케이크 가루에 굴리면서 묻혀낸다.

∗ 케이크는 집에서 분량대로 구워 다 부스러뜨려 가루를 만들든지 상점에서 구입해서 가루를 만들면 되고, 곱게 가루를 만들고 싶으면 고운 채에 받쳐서 거르면 덩어리지지 않고 아주 곱게 된다.

∗ 케이크는 어떤 종류라도 좋다.

∗ 찹쌀가루, 통조림 팥앙금은 동양식품에서 구입.

6 servings

1 lb. glutinous rice flour* (Koda Farms, Japanese brand), 1½ cup water, 1 lb. sweetened red bean paste* (available in a can), 3 cups cake crumbs, 20 cups water for boiling dumplings

Making

Mix the rice flour with water to make a dough, shape it into a long log, then cut into walnut size pieces. Roll each piece into a 3″ circle and put a teaspoonful of red bean paste in the center. Then gather up the edges and pinch together with your fingers to seal and shape the dumpling into a ball.

Drop five dumplings at a time into boiling water and cook until they rise to the surface. Remove with a slotted spoon and shake off any excess water. Roll the dumpling in cake crumbs to fully coat. Repeat the process for each dumpling.

∗ Note : Cake crumbs, available at bakeries, can be made at home by crumbling day old cake of any kind; sift for finer crumbs.

∗ Available in Asian groceries.

별 · 미 · 요 · 리 (Specials)

구절판 (Korean Hord' Oeuvres, Gujeolpan)

🍲 준비는 이렇게(5인분)

쇠고기 ¼ lb., 오이 3개, 표고버섯 10개, 밀가루 1 컵, 죽순(통조림 1개) 혹은 도라지, 당근 2개, 양파 3개, 계란 5개, 물 1¼ 컵

🍲 만드는 것은 이렇게

❶ 쇠고기는 포를 떠서 갖은 양념을 하여 오븐에 구워서 채썬다.
❷ 오이는 2인치 길이로 잘라 길이로 껍질을 벗겨 채로 썰어 소금에 절인 후 물기를 없애고 식용유에 볶는다.
❸ 당근과 양파도 채로 썰어 식용유에 살짝 볶으면서 소금과 설탕으로 간을 맞춘다.
❹ 죽순은 채썰어 식용유를 넣고 볶는다.(도라지를 쓸 때는 곱게 찢어서 식용유에 볶으면서 고기국물을 한 국자 넣고 뭉근하게 볶는다.)
❺ 버섯은 2, 3일전에 물에 담가놓았다가 깨끗이 씻어서 채썰어 식용유에 볶는다.
❻ 계란은 황백으로 갈라 지단을 부친다.(녹말가루와 소금을 약간 넣어 부친다.)
❼ 밀가루는 분량대로 개어 얇게 밀전병으로 부친다.(소금을 조금 넣는다.)
❽ 이상의 재료들을 구절판에 구색을 맞추어 담아 내놓고 초장, 초고추장, 겨자, 간장을 곁들여 식성에 맞추어 먹는다.

🍲 양념 준비는 이렇게

파, 마늘, 생강, 간장, 참기름, 설탕, 소금,후추
＊각 야채를 볶을 때 식용유는 ½큰술, 소금은 약간 (¼작은술) 넣음

🍲 5 servings

Prepare each vegetable ingredient separately using a little cooking oil and a dash of salt. 1 cup flour, 3 cucumbers, seedless, cut in strips, lightly stir-fried per above instructions., 2 carrots, peeled, cut in strips, lightly stir-fried per above, 3 onions, sliced vertically to make strips, stir-fried per above, 10 black mushrooms, soften in water, cut in strips, stir-fried per above, 1 cup bamboo shoots* (canned), rinsed, cut in strips, stir-fried per above, 2 tsp. cornstarch, 5 egg whites, lightly beaten with cornstarch and a dash of salt, cooked in a heated, greased skillet, spread evenly to make 2 thin pancakes, then cut in thin strips, 5 egg yolks, lightly beaten with 2 teaspoons water, fried and cut per egg whites,¼ lb. beef, thinly sliced, marinated in mixture below, broiled, cut in strips, cooking oil, salt, water

🍲 Making

Mix the flour with 1¼ cup water and a dash of salt to make a thin batter. Fry per the egg whites to make 5-6 large pancakes. Using a cookie cutter or the rim of a glass, cut the pancakes into circles to fit your serving dish, preferably a Koo Jeul Pahn server. Combine the marinade ingredients.
To serve, place the pancake circles in the center of the Koo Jeul Pahn or a large, flat serving platter and attractively arrange the other ingredients in the 8 surrounding sections. Diners then place the ingredients of their choice on a pancake, roll it up and enjoy.

🍲 For marinade

1 tbsp. soy sauce, 1 tbsp. sugar, 1 tsp. minced garlic, ¼ tsp. grated ginger, 1 tbsp. sesame oil, ¼ tsp. black pepper, 1 tsp. spring onion, chopped

＊Note : As a substitute for bamboo shoots, try a cup of doh-ra-ji*, soakedin water until soft, cut in thin strips, stir-fried, then simmered in 2tablespoons meat broth until soft enough to serve.
＊Available in Asian groceries.

별 · 미 · 요 · 리 (Specials)

꾼만두 구이 (Pan-fried Dumplings)

🍲 준비는 이렇게(5인분)

만두피 2팩(50장×2), 쇠고기 다진 것 ½ lb., 다진 당면 1.8 oz., 다진 캬베츠 1컵, 다진 파 1컵, 호박 1컵 (다짐), 당근 ½ cup (다짐), 송이버섯 4 oz (다짐), 달걀 흰자 1개

🍲 만드는 것은 이렇게

❶ 위의 재료중 호박다짐에 소금 ¼작은술을 넣어 물기를 꼭 뺀다.
❷ 캬베츠 다짐에 식초, 소금, 설탕에 절여 물기를 꼭 짠다.(식초 ½작은술, 설탕 1작은술, 소금 ¼작은술)
❸ 쇠고기는 절반은 생으로 쓰고 절반은 후추 약간 뿌려 쿠킹와인을 넣고 볶는다.
❹ 당면은 푹 삶아 다 익으면 잘게 다져둔다. 송이버섯, 당근, 파도 각각 잘게 다진다.
❺ 준비된 모든 재료를 한데 넣고 양념을 넣어 골고루 잘 버무린다. 이 때 달걀 흰자를 넣는다.

* 설탕과 식초, 소금은 캬베츠 절이는 데만 넣는다.
* 달걀 노른자에 물 3큰술 넣고 만두피에 발라 만들어 놓은 속을 넣고 위를 꼭꼭 눌러 만두를 빚는다.
* 프라이팬에 기름을 2큰술 붓고 만두를 판판하게 놓고 센불에서 점점 약한 불로 조절하면서 노릇노릇 굽는다.
* 튀김 만두를 원하면 식용유(3컵)를 판판한 냄비에 붓고 기름이 끓어오를 때 빚어 놓은 만두를 넣는다. 튀겨낼 때 타지 않도록 불 조절을 잘해야 한다.

🍲 만두속 양념은 이렇게

볶은깨 4큰술, 참기름 2큰술, 후추¼작은술, 기꼬망 간장 1큰술, 식초 ½작은술, 쿠킹와인 ½작은술, 설탕 1작은술, 소금마늘가루½작은술

🍲 5 servings

1 tsp. salt, 1 tsp. sugar, 1 tsp. vinegar, 1 cup cabbage, chopped, ½ lb. ground beef, ¼ tsp. black pepper, ½ tsp. cooking wine, 1.8 oz. transparent noodles, boiled, drained and chopped, 1 cup spring onions, chopped, 1 cup zucchini, chopped, sprinkled with salt and any liquid squeezed out, ½ cup carrots, chopped finely, 4 oz. black mushrooms, softened in water, liquid gently squeezed out, chopped, 1 egg white, 4 tbsp. toasted sesame seeds, 2 tbsp. sesame oil, 1 tbsp. soy sauce, 2 pkgs. wonton wrappers (50 per package), 1 egg yolk, 3 tbsp. water, 2 tbsp. cooking oil

🍲 Making

To make the filling, sprinkle salt, sugar and vinegar over cabbage, let stand for a few minutes, then squeeze out all liquid. Brown half the ground beef with a dash of black pepper and the cooking wine. Add the remaining beef, the cabbage and the next nine listed ingredients (except wonton wrappers, egg yolk, water and cooking oil) and gently but thoroughly mix.

Line up wonton wrappers on a large cutting board and brush the edges with a mixture of one egg yolk and 3 tablespoons water. Place a small amount of the filling mixture on a wrapper, gather the edges to the center and pinch to seal the filling inside the dumpling. Continue the process and fill each wrapper. Heat the cooking oil in a heavy skillet. Add dumplings in small batches and brown lightly until done, adjusting the heat from high to low.

팥죽 (Red Bean Soup with Dumplings)

준비는 이렇게(4인분)

팥 340g (12oz), 물 2 Ltr., 베이킹소다 ¼작은술, 찹쌀가루 2 컵, 소금 1½ 작은술, 물 1½컵

만드는 것은 이렇게

❶ 팥 340g에 물 2리터를 붓고 베이킹소다를 넣고 물기가 하나도 없을 때까지(40분~45분 정도) 센불에 끓인다.

❷ 팥이 완전히 삶아지면 아주 부드럽고 연하다.

❸ 팥 3½ 컵에 물 4컵을 부어 믹서기에 두 번 나누어 간 후 고운 채에 거른 뒤 건더기 남은 팥 3½ 컵에 물 2 컵을 넣어서 한번 더 믹서에 간 다음 한꺼번에 냄비에 붓고 끓인다. (알맹이 하나 도 없이 완전히 고운 가루죽이 됨.)

❹ 한참 20분 정도 끓이다가 부글부글 소리나면 찹쌀가루 ½컵에 물 ½ 컵을 타서 끓고 있는 팥죽에 같이 넣어 걸쭉하게 끓인다. (나무주걱으로 계속 잘 저어야 된다.)

찹쌀 새알(동그라미) 만들기는 이렇게

❶ 찹쌀가루 1½ 컵에 물 1컵으로 반죽하여 새알을 만든다.

❷ 찹쌀새알을 끓는 팥죽에 넣는다.

❸ 다 익으면 새알(동그라미)이 위로 뜬다.

❹ 그때 소금 1½작은술을 넣고 싱거우면 조심성있게 조금씩 조금씩 더 넣는다.

＊ 경우에 따라서 찹쌀가루 대신 불린 쌀을 넣을 수도 있다.

＊ 찹쌀가루는 일본제 모찌꼬 가루 (KODA
  FARMS에서 나온 16oz(1lb)
  Box에 들어 있다.〉

4 servings

2 cups glutinous rice flour (1 lb. Koda Farms brand), 12 oz. dried red beans*, ¼ tsp. baking soda, 1½ tsp. salt, water

Making

Combine 1½ cups rice flour with 1 cup of water to make a dough. Roll teaspoon sized pieces of dough between your hands and shape into round marble size dumplings.

In a large saucepan over high heat, cook the red beans with baking soda in 2 liters of water until soft and the water is nearly all absorbed, about 40-45 minutes. In a food processor, puree the bean mixture with 6 cups of water to a thick consistency. To make it creamy, strain the puree through a fine colander into a saucepan.

Heat the bean mixture to a boil. Add the dumplings. When the dumplings are cooked, they will rise to the surface. Thicken with ½ cup rice flour mixed with ½ cup water. Adjust the seasoning with salt and serve.

＊Available in Asian groceries.

잣죽 (Creamy Pine Nut Soup)

🥣 준비는 이렇게(3인분)

잣 ½컵, 쌀 ¾컵, 물 3컵, 소금 1½작은술

🥣 만드는 것은 이렇게

❶ 잣과 쌀을 같이 물 3컵을 붓고 5시간 이상 불린 뒤에 믹서기에 간다.

❷ 믹서에 한번 갈아 채에 받쳐서 거른 뒤에 건더기를 물 ½컵과 같이 다시 믹서에 넣고 한번 더 갈고 거른다. 거른 국물 1컵을 남은 건더기와 같이 한번 더 간 뒤에 거르고 남은 찌꺼기는 버린다.

❸ 납작한 냄비에 국물 전체를 붓고 나무주걱으로 젓는다.

❹ 팔팔 끓으면 소금 1½작은술을 넣고 빡빡하면 물 2큰술을 붓는다. 식성에 따라 물을 조금씩 더 부어도 된다.

🥣 3 servings

½ cup pine nuts, ¾ cup rice, 4½ cups water, 1½ tsp. salt

🥣 Making

  Soak pine nuts and rice in water for 5 hours, then puree in a food processor until creamy. Line a colander with a double layer of cheese cloth and strain pureed mixture into a saucepan. Discard the residue. Cook the soup, stirring constantly. When boiling, add salt and dilute with two or more tablespoons water to obtain the desired consistency.

별 · 미 · 요 · 리 (Specials)

수정과 (Ginger Flavored Persimmon Dessert)

준비는 이렇게 (8인분)

곶감 8개, 생강(납작썰기) ½컵, 물 14컵, 잣 조금, 통계피 6개, 흑설탕 1컵

만드는 것은 이렇게

❶ 물 14컵에 생강 썬 것 ½컵을 넣고 매운 냄새가 날 때까지 끓인다.(끓고부터 10분 정도까지)

❷ 생강물의 반을 나누어 통계피를 넣고 같이 끓인다.(끓고부터 5분), 한소끔 끓여 식힌 뒤에 곶감 8개를 넣고 생강은 건어내버리고 통계피는 곶감과 같이 담가둔다. 이때 흑설탕 1컵을 넣는다.

＊ 식힌 뒤에 냉장고에 두었다가 상에 낼 때 잣을 띄운다.

8 servings

8 dried persimmons*, ½ cup ginger slices, 14 cups water, 6 cinnamon sticks, 1 cup brown sugar, pine nuts for garnish

Making

In a pot, boil the water with the ginger about 10 minutes or until a strong ginger fragrance emerges. To half of this ginger water, add the cinnamon sticks and bring to a boil. Let cool a bit, discard the ginger, add the persimmons and the remaining half of the ginger water, including any cinnamon sticks in it, then add the brown sugar. Store in the refrigerator. Garnish with pine nuts when serving.

＊Available in Asian groceries.

별 · 미 · 요 · 리 (Specials)

귤 · 배 · 생강차 (Ginger Tea with Pear and Orange)

준비는 이렇게(6인분)

귤 2개, 생강(납작썰기) ½컵, 물 12컵, 배 1개, 흰설탕 ⅓컵, 딸기 약간

만드는 것은 이렇게

❶ 귤은 껍질을 잘 씻어 깎아놓는다. 생강은 납작납작 썰고 배는 ⅔를 반달형으로 큼직큼직하게 껍질째 썰어 놓는다.

❷ 남은 배는 껍질을 벗기고 모양찍기로 꽃모양으로 떠놓는다.

❸ 물 12컵에 귤껍질과 생강 썬 것을 같이 넣고 끓인다. 끓기 시작해서 10 분 후 불을 끄면서 깎아놓은 귤알맹이와 껍질째 썰어 놓은 배, 설탕 ⅓컵을 넣는다.

❹ 그대로 냉장고에 두고 하룻밤을 지난 뒤 물만 남기고 배, 귤껍질, 귤, 생강은 건어내 버린다.

❺ 상에 낼 때 깨끗한 유리컵에 꽃모양 빚은 배와 납작 썬 딸기를 3~4개 띄운다.

* 겨울철 건강에 매우 좋으며, 감기예방에 아주 좋다.

6 servings

2 oranges, ½ cup ginger, sliced, 12 cups water, 1 pear, ⅔ unpeeled and sliced, ⅓ cut in a flower shape for garnish, ⅓ cup sugar, strawberry slices for garnish

Making

Carefully peel off the orange rind, reserving the fruit. Put the rind, water and ginger in a pot and boil 10 minutes, then remove the pot from the heat. Cut the orange sections in halves, and add them, the ⅔ unpeeled pear slices and sugar to the pot and refrigerate overnight. The next day, strain and serve cold. Garnish with a flower shaped pear and slices of strawberry.

* Note : This tea can also be served hot and is thought to be a preventative for colds.

겨자채
(Seafood Salad with Mustard Dressing)

불고기
(Korean Barbeque Beef)

골뱅이 해초무침
(Conch and Fresh Kelp Salad)

생강 닭요리
(Ginger Chicken)

황백생선전 · 게살전
(Pan Fried Yellow and White Fish Slices)

오색배추모듬이
(Five Color Rolls)

오렌지 쇠고기요리
(Orange Beef)

매운 새우와 매운 조개
(Spicy Shrimp and Scallops)

오징어 강정
(Fried Squid Dish)

닭고기 보쌈
(Lettuce Wrapped Chicken)

모듬초밥
(Assorted Seafood Sushi)

막기김밥
(Rolled Sushi)

봄, 여름, 가을, 겨울, 사계절에 손님초대 경우 구분별 메뉴 중에서 4~5개 정도 요리를 뽑아 메뉴를 정하고 그때 맞는 나물과 토속 조림과 김치를 정해 12가지 정도 색 맞추어 상을 차리면 어렵지 않고 훌륭한 계절 상차림이 된다.

Pick just a few recipes from different sections of this book. A beautiful, nutritious, twelve - color meal can be created.
Add a few fresh seasonal vegetable dishes and kimchi.

황백생선전

오징어 강정

겨자채

오색냉소면
(Five-Colors Cold Noodle Dish)

불고기
(Korean Barbeque Beef)

8색 미역 냉채
(Colorful Seaweed Salad)

국수곁들인 낙지볶음
(Stir-fried Octopus with Noodles)

해파리 냉채
(Cold with Jellyfish Salad)

오징어 야채무침
(Squid Salad)

겨자채
(Seafood Salad with Mustard Dressing)

돼지불고기
(Spicy Barbeque Pork)

오색 배추 모듬말이
(Five Color Rolls)

막기김밥
(Rolled Sushi)

모듬초밥
(Assorted Seafood Sushi)

꽃다발김밥
(California Roll)

모듬초밥

오색소면 전골
(Colorful Hot Pot with Noodles)

배즙 갈비찜
(Stewed Beef Ribs with Pear Juice)

생강 닭요리
(Ginger Chicken)

양장피 잡채
(Salad with Mungbean Starch Sheet)

해물파전
(Pan Fried Spring Onion Patties with Seafood)

쇠고기탕수육
(Sweet and Sour Beef)

아구찜
(Braised Monk Fish)

떡볶이
(Stir-fried Rice Cake)

잡채
(Transparent Noodles with Vegetables)

낙지·버섯·새우쌈요리
(Lettuce Wrapped Seafood)

모듬초밥
(Assorted Seafood Sushi)

막기김밥
(Rolled Sushi)

오뎅 야채 우동 전골
(Hot Pot with Fishcake, Vegetables and Noodles)

◆

갈비찜
(Stewed Beef Ribs)

◆

생강 닭요리
(Ginger Chicken)

◆

잡채
(Transparent Noodles with Vegetables)

◆

해물파전
(Pan Fried Spring Onion Patties with Seafood)

◆

해파리냉채
(Cold with Jellyfish Salad)

탕수육
(Sweet and Sour Beef)

◆

팔보채
(Eight Treasures Dish)

◆

왕만두전골
(Stuffed Giant Dumplings)

◆

떡볶이
(Stir-Fried Rice Cake)

◆

꽃다발 김밥
(California Roll)

◆

해삼탕
(Sea Cucumber Dish)

팔보채

떡볶이

오뎅 · 야채 · 우동전골

WEIGHTS AND MEASURES

Weight and measures

1 lbs = 454g

1 cup = 200g

1 cup = 13 1/3 tbsp.

1 cup = 40 tsp.

1 tbsp. = 15g

1 tsp. = 5g

Grain

1 cup rice = 180g

1 cup Barley = 170g

1 cup flour = 120g

1 cup bean = 180g

1 cup red bean = 150g

1 cup Mung bean = 160g

1 cup starch = 120g

1 tbsp. starch = 7g

Sauces and condiments

1 tbsp. chili bean paste = 15g

1 tbsp. bean paste = 18g

1 tbsp. soy bean sauce = 18g

1 cup hot chili powder = 100g

1 tbsp. sesame oil = 15g

1 tbsp. roasted sesame seed = 6g

1 tbsp. vegetable oil = 13g

재료의 어림치와 무게

계량단위

1컵	200g
1큰술	15g
1작은술	5g
1컵	13⅓큰술(40작은술)

곡류

쌀 1컵	180g
통보리쌀 1컵	170g
밀가루 1컵	120g
콩 1컵	180g
팥 1컵	150g
차조 · 수수 · 녹두 1컵	160g
녹말가루 1컵	120g
녹말가루 1큰술	7g

양념류

고추장 1큰술	15g
된장 1큰술	18g
간장1큰술	18g
고춧가루 1컵	100g
참기름 1큰술	15g
깨소금 1큰술	6g
식물성 기름 1큰술	13g